# The Modern Crusaders

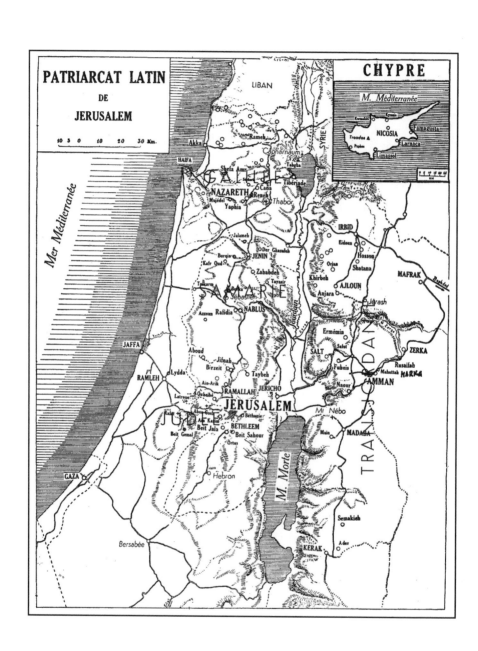

PATRIARCAT LATIN
DE
JERUSALEM

10 5 0    10    20    30 Km.

CHYPRE

M. Méditerranée

NICOSIA
Famagusta
Kyrenia
Troodos ▲
Pathos
Larnaca
Limassol

Mer Méditerranée

LIBAN

SYRIE

HAIFA
Akka
Rameh
Capharnaüm
Tabgha
Shefa Amr
GALILEE
Tibériade
NAZARETH
Cana
Reneh
Mujédel
Yaphia
Thabor

IRBID
Eidoun
Jalameh
Hosson
Der Ghazaleh
Burqin
JENIN
Orjan
Shatana
Kafr Qud
Zababdeh
Khirbeh
Tayair
MAFRAK
AJLOUN
Tolkarm
SAMARIE
Anjara
Sebastieh
Jerash
Rafidia
NABLUS
Azzoun

JAFFA

Aboud
Ermémin
Jifnah
SALT
Safut
ZERKA
Birzeit
Taybeh
Rusaifah
Ain-Arik
Fuheis
Mahattah  MARKA
RAMLEH
Lydda
Naour
AMMAN
Qubeibe
RAMALLAH
JERICHO
Latroun
Abou Ghoch
Béthanie
Mr Nébo
JUDEE
Beit Jala
Abou Karim
BETHLEEM
MADABA
Beit Gemal
Beit Sahour
Main
Ortas

GAZA
Hebron
M. Morte
TRANSJORDAN

Semakieh
Bersabée
Ader
KERAK

# The Modern Crusaders

*A Brief History of the Equestrian Order*
*of the Holy Sepulchre of Jerusalem*

by
## SIR ALFRED J. BLASCO
### KNIGHT OF THE COLLAR

With emendations by
Sir Duane A. Burchick, Sr., KHS
under the direction of
H.E. Sir Bernard J. Ficarra, KGCHS
Middle Atlantic Lieutenancy

*PenRose*
Publishing Company
P.O. Box 620
Mystic Island, New Jersey 08087

# Dedication

*To*
*His Eminence*
*Joseph Cardinal Caprio*
*Cardinal Grand Master Emeritus of the*
*Equestrian Order of the Holy Sepulchre of Jerusalem*
*this book is humbly and gratefully dedicated in appreciation of his*
*inspiring leadership and untiring service to the Order.*

# Acknowledgments

The completion of a book is customarily the occasion for a profusion of thanks and expressions of indebtedness to all those without whom the book could not have been written. In this particular case it is no exaggeration as the book could not have been written without the friendship, support, and help in many and varied ways that came from numerous individuals: Ronald E. Prosser, K.M.I., K.C.N., historian; Sir Truman Stacey, KCHS, at the Office of Communications of the Lake Charles Diocese; Reverend P. Medebielle, S.J., of the seminary at Beit Jala near Bethlehem; His Excellency the late Knight of the Collar, Sir Douglas Jenkins, former Lieutenant of England and Wales, who, in particular, offered valuable suggestions and help; and Honorable Marcel Dingli-Attard, Consul of Malta.

I am very much indebted to His Excellency, Sir F. Russell Kendall, Knight of the Collar, Vice Governor General of the Equestrian Order of the Holy Sepulchre of Jerusalem, for going over the draft. His support during its preparation is especially appreciated. I am also indebted to the Lieutenants of the United States, Canada, and Mexico for their cooperation in furnishing information on their Lieutenancies. I also want to thank Sister Marie Eschbacher, L.S.J., Ph.D., retired Education Department Head of Avila College, for editing this book. I am most grateful for her help and guidance as the manuscript went into several revisions and for the sense of humor she was able to retain throughout.

After an initial setback towards publication, His Excellency, Sir Bernard J. Ficarra picked up the cross, directed the emendation of the final version, edited the entire document, and ushered the draft through the detailed review and approval by the Grand Magisterium. Under his command, Sir Duane A. Burchick, Sr., KHS, did a beautiful job of emendating the entire manuscript while contributing Part III on "Ideal Chivalry." The final document frankly surpasses the original manuscript.

While the friendship and support offered has been vital and indispensable to the completion of this book, I alone am responsible for what I have written, and all possible errors and faults in this book are mine

*A.J.B.*

# Contents

# Illustrations

# Foreword

The illustrious history of the Equestrian Order of the Holy Sepulchre of Jerusalem from its founding in 1099 by Godfrey de Bouillon to the present is the story of unbroken service to the Catholic Church, Christianity, and humanity in general. The spirit and objectives of the valiant Christian nobleman, who occasioned the Order, have traditionally guided its activities within religious, charitable, and social institutions. Schools, hospitals, dispensaries, and asylums, associated with the mission of the Latin Patriarch of Jerusalem, have been its beneficiaries. Today, the affirmation of the Christian character of the Holy Land, made sacred by the association with the birth, life, and death of Jesus Christ, is tragically needed.

As the twentieth century of Christianity comes to a close, we can reflect on the repetition of human experiences that cry out for justice and charity. The environment has changed as invention has dramatically increased the possibilities for a greater good, but ill will unfortunately has denied these opportunities to many. We know from the teachings of Vatican II that the fruits of science must be shared and the common good be foremost in the mind and heart of man.

Knights and Ladies of the Holy Sepulchre are enlisted in a new crusade with the armament of prayer, example, and charity. The crusade is of multipurpose, but two purposes stand out: one, to change the fading presence of Christians in the Holy Land and the threat to the sacred shrines of Christianity and, two, to relieve the neglected poor in the Holy Land who struggle for life itself.

The noble purpose that motivated James the Apostle, St. Helena, Charlemagne, and Godfrey of Bouillon is embraced today. The strength of the effort derives from faith in God and its success in the dedication of faithful Knights and Ladies. The poor are powerless, and this truth was never more manifest than in the condition of the poor in the Holy Land. Knights and Ladies must help them.

The shrines of Christianity are slowly becoming museums as Christian Palestinians are forced to emigrate from their homeland. The stones that pressed the feet of Christ and the apostles must be preserved as sacred with the same fervor evinced by Christian champions and martyrs of days past. Knights and Ladies must see to this.

The Order accepts its mission and mandate in a spirit of knightly and evangelical dedication. It strives to help the Christian community in the Holy Land endure and perform its duties as a community of faith. In so doing, the Knights and Ladies of the Holy Sepulchre are modern crusaders. **God wills it!**

It is the desire of the author that this slim volume will aid in the understanding of the purpose of these Christian men and women. While my description of the organization that provides this common bond is brief, the author trusts that it shows the continuity of the Order and the relatedness of its goals to the present.

# I

# The Holy Land and the Equestrian Order of the Holy Sepulchre of Jerusalem

*The sacred armies, and the godly knight,*
*That the great sepulchre of Christ did free,*
*I sing; much wrought his valor and foresight,*
*And in that glorious war much suffered he;*
*In vain 'gainst him did Hell oppose her might,*
*In vain the Turks and Morians armed be:*
*His soldiers wild, to brawls and mutinies prest,*
*Reduced he to peace, so Heaven him blest.*

*Jerusalem Delivered* by Torquato Tasso (1544–1595)
translated by Edward Fairfax (1560–1635)
First Book, Stanza I

# CHAPTER 1

# THE HOLY LAND

The Holy Land, no larger than the state of Vermont, honored as the land in which Jesus Christ was born, lived, died, and was buried, was a small Roman province situated at the junction of three great divisions of the world—Asia, Africa, and Europe. Palestine, as this country was called in ancient times, runs north and south for one hundred and twenty-five miles, varying in width from twenty-five to seventy-five miles. It is bounded on the north by the foothills of Lebanon, on the West by the Mediterranean, and on the East by the Valley of Jordan. Its southern extremity is triangular in shape, with the point extending southward to the Gulf of Aquaba, the western side being bounded by the Peninsula of Sinai and the eastern side by the mountains of Transjordan. This is now all a part of Israel except for the west bank of the Jordan River and the Gaza Strip. In the time of Our Lord, Palestine was divided into four provinces: Judea, Samaria, Galilee, and Perea.

As the site of numerous Old and New Testament events, the Holy Land has remained a cherished land to all who value their Judeo-Christian heritage—particularly to Knights and Ladies of the Order of the Holy Sepulchre of Jerusalem. This is the site of the Holy Sepulchre—the source and origin of the Order. This most venerated spot has been an object of pilgrimage and piety from the time of the Apostles. The Christian community of Jerusalem was often persecuted under Roman rule, as we learn from the Acts of the Apostles, so public worship at the spot was limited.

Constantine, the first Christian Emperor of Rome, changed all that. He built a Roman basilica to mark the sacred place. This structure was set in four parts: an atrium at the head of the steps from the main street, a basilica, an open courtyard containing the Rock of Golgotha, and the Holy Sepulchre itself, surmounted by a dome supported by columns with silver capitals, known as the "Anastasis," or Church of the Resurrection. Begun in 326 A.D., this complex was dedicated in 335 A.D. The work on the tomb was not quite finished at the dedication because of the immense labor involved in cutting away the cliff in order to isolate the tomb-chamber. This was completed sometime before 348 A.D.

Jerusalem remained a Christian community until 638 A.D. when it was taken from the Roman Empire by the Moslems. Jerusalem declined in importance under Moslem rule, but an influx of Moslem settlers did much to kindle hatred among the various religious communities in the city. In 939, and again in 966, Moslems attacked Christians and burned the church of the Holy Sepulchre and other churches. On the latter occasion, when the Muslim attackers were joined by the Jews, the

*"Peter the Hermit Preaching the Crusade"*
Gustav Doré (1832–1883) from *The History of the Crusades*
by Joseph François Michaud (1767–1839)

Christian Patriarch was murdered and his body burned. Pious pilgrims and local Christians partially restored the church, but it was destroyed again by the Fatimid Caliph, Al-Hakim, in 1009. The Church remained in ruins until the Byzantine emperor paid for its restoration in 1048. But only the Church of the Resurrection was rebuilt. The basilica of Constantine lay in ruins.

This was the situation in 1099 when the soldiers of the First Crusade led by Godfrey de Bouillon captured the city. Godfrey refused to accept the title "King of Jerusalem" in deference to Christ, and instead took the title "Advocate of the Holy Sepulchre." Laying his sword before the Holy Sepulchre, he pledged to God to defend the holy site with his life. He immediately set up a contingent of his best knights to guard the site from any further desecration. The Order of the Holy Sepulchre, as the guardian knights began calling themselves, soon found itself with additional duties and was to be drawn into the two-hundred year war to preserve the Kingdom of Jerusalem.

Unfortunately, soon after the conquest of Jerusalem, most of the great barons of Europe, who had taken a vow to redeem the Holy Sepulchre, departed to Europe with their knights and men-at-arms. They considered that they had fulfilled their vow and were free to withdraw. Godfrey and a few others were left with the task of maintaining the kingdom that would keep Jerusalem and the other Christian holy places open to the pilgrims of Europe. This was a task given to the few to stand against the many. It was a most heroic challenge that was met with superb dedication and served as the chivalric model for centuries. It was a great loss when Godfrey died in 1100, scarcely a year after he had led the way into the city.

Upon Godfrey's death, his brother Baldwin was elected to succeed him and did not scruple to take the title "King of Jerusalem." Upon accepting the crown, he also assumed the grand mastership of the Order of the Holy Sepulchre. By 1113, the guardian order had advanced to the point that Pope Paschal II approved and recognized the Knights of the Holy Sepulchre as a Military Order. More and more knights were inducted into the Order, constantly on guard against Muslim attempts to retake the city. Baldwin held the grand mastership until his death in 1118, and thereafter, the successive kings of Jerusalem assumed control. Thus the deeds of the Order are chronicled under the acts of the king until the Crusaders were finally driven from their last stronghold, Acre, in 1291.

One of the most permanent legacies of the Crusaders was a reconstructed Church of the Holy Sepulchre. This crusader church, which still stands, was built to cover both the site of the crucifixion and the site of the tomb of Christ, and thus incorporated a number of other structures within its confines. This new church was dedicated in 1149, exactly 50 years after the conquest of Jerusalem. It is to this church that present-day Knights and Ladies of the Order go to pray when they make their pilgrimage to the Holy Land.

The Crusades, one of the great social movements of the Middle Ages, gave a galvanizing impulse to the institution of knighthood. New ideas of discipline and dedication were born. The religious fervor that resulted in the launching of armies of western soldiers against the Muslims of the Middle East, did not subside once the walls of Jerusalem were breached. Within months of the conquest, monks were becoming soldiers and soldiers were becoming monks. It was at this time that the great religious orders of knighthood came into being. These new associations took upon themselves the "rule" of St. Benedict, or of one of the other orders of monks, and became brethren bound by the triple monastic vows of poverty, celibacy, and obedience. Moreover, they were bound by an additional vow to shed their blood in the defense of the True Faith.

Today, Catholics are no longer asked to die but to live for the Holy Land. They are no longer asked to use arms to defend the Holy Places, but to use every legitimate peaceful means to safeguard the rights and the interests of the Church in that Sacred Place. Knights and Ladies of the Order are asked to *collaborate with those responsible for the interests of the Church in the Holy Land to enable them* to carry on successfully the religious and sacred work that preserves the Living Christian Faith and, above all, the glory of God and the good of the people.

*Church of the Holy Sepulchre*

# CHAPTER 2

# ORIGIN OF THE ORDER

Among the ancient chivalric orders, the Equestrian Order of the Holy Sepulchre of Jerusalem occupies an extraordinary and exalted position, having been chosen to guard the most sacred spot in the Holy City of Jerusalem, and, indeed, in all of Christendom, the tomb of Christ. The Order is an ecclesiastical Roman Catholic Order of ancient lineage, rich tradition, and history. It has enjoyed the benevolent protection and the high favor of the Holy See. The historic mission of the Order is to support the preservation and propagation of the Faith and the protection of the Catholic Church in the Holy Land.

The Order of the Holy Sepulchre is of such antiquity that the details of its origin are disputed among scholars. There are four names that are associated with precursors to and the actual laying of the foundation that gave rise to the Order. The three forerunners are the apostle, St. James The Less, the Roman emperor's mother St. Helena and the Holy Roman Emperor Charlemagne. A fourth stands out clearly as the chivalric source: the first overlord of the Crusader States, Godfrey de Bouillon.

St. James the Apostle was, according to tradition, a cousin of Jesus Christ, and was the first Bishop of Jerusalem. He rallied a number of disciples under the standard of the Cross to guard the Holy Tomb. This group was the first to accept the holy charge, and were known as Canons of the Holy Sepulchre.

More than 200 years after the death of St. James, another great figure appeared on the scene—one who is remembered most because of her association with Jerusalem—St. Helena, wife of Constantius, a Roman General, and mother of Constantine the Great. After defeating his rival Maxentius in 312, Constantine with his ally Licinius became co-emperors. In 313, he and Licinius met in Milan and issued the Edict of Milan, confirming an earlier edict issued in 309 which stated that Christianity would be tolerated throughout the Roman Empire—a turning point for Christianity. Helena came to Jerusalem and is credited with the discovery of the true relic of the Cross on which Christ was crucified. With the construction of the Church of the Holy Sepulchre, Helena established a guard of mace-bearers to watch the Tomb by day and by night.

Some scholars have said that Charlemagne, the restorer of the Holy Roman Empire, founded the Order of the Holy Sepulchre. It is definitely known that he did establish an Order of the Crown of Charlemagne, and many of his tenets were later adopted and observed by the Knights of the Holy Sepulchre. Moreover, during his stay in Rome in 800, in the presence of Pope Leo III, he received the representatives

*Godfrey de Boullion (1060–1100) Advocatus Sancti Sepulchri*
*Portrait by Jeronimo de Espinosa (1600–1680) Spanish School*

of the Patriarch of Jerusalem who delivered to him the keys of the Holy Sepulchre, of the hill of Calvary, of the Holy City, and, also, a testament to his sovereignty.

About two centuries later, the world learned of another great and reverent person, Godfrey de Bouillon, who was born in Belgium. Godfrey was to find a much larger world to be his field of action when, in 1096, he answered the call of Pope Urban II to lead a crusade. After two years and enormous difficulties, he and his crusading forces took the city of Jerusalem. The Order of the Holy Sepulchre can definitely trace its existence to the time when Godfrey set out to wrest the Holy City from the occupation of the infidels.

While many opinions exist as to the origin of the Order, all agree with the insignia of these Knights. This was worn on the breast and consisted of a red cross on a white background, with four smaller crosses placed in each corner. This form of cross represents the five wounds of Our Savior from which, as from so many precious fountains, flows the stream of salvation for humanity.

It is, however, in 1099, with the capture of Jerusalem that the history of the Order emerges from the uncertainty of legend. It was natural that the Christian warriors who had braved so much to free the holy places from Muslim domination should desire to receive the tokens of knighthood in the Church of the Holy Sepulchre, and that they should feel a special devotion to this very sacred place. Those knights who received their investiture at the Holy Sepulchre itself, and who constituted a guard of honor at the shrine, were approved as an order in a Bull of Approbation by Pope Paschal II in 1113.

As early as 1125, recorded acts of Papal confirmation and recognition of the Order are to be found. The Knights of the Holy Sepulchre adopted the Rule of St. Augustine and assumed the guardianship of the Tomb of Our Savior. Other orders of knighthood were similarly born, each with its own special functions. The order entrusted with the care and protection of the Temple accepted the austere Rule of the Cistercians. They were called Knights Templars. The Knights of Saint Lazare, who followed the rule of St. Basil, undertook to care for lepers. The Hospitallers of St. John of Jerusalem, later and to this day known as the Knights of Malta, cared for the sick and the strangers in Jerusalem while adopting the Rule of St. Augustine. Of these orders only the Order of the Holy Sepulchre and the Order of Malta have survived in an unbroken succession from their founding until the present day. The Order of Malta is today a sovereign order, having all the attributes of sovereignty within itself and with ultimate authority in its own appointed grand master. It enjoys the patronage of the Holy See. The Order of the Holy Sepulchre, on the other hand, is an ecclesiastical Order and is part of the Holy See with the Pope as its Supreme Head, under whose personal protection it thrives.

The history of the Knights of the Holy Sepulchre comes down through the corridors of time for nearly a millennium. The world today is somewhat different from that era in which the original brave and noble knights of the Cross lived. Yet the work of the knights is not finished: Our Lord still needs us.

# CHAPTER 3

# THE ORDER DURING THE CRUSADES

The Knights of the Holy Sepulchre formed the spearhead of a formidable military force that in spite of the necessity to fight many battles against the Saracens enabled the new Kingdom of Jerusalem to thrive for nearly a hundred years. The Knights were uniquely associated with the King: the King was the Grand Master of the Order, while the Latin Patriarch was the Grand Prior. This association foreshadowed the future subordination to the Supreme Pontiff. Both the King and the Patriarch could invest knights, and in the absence of the King, the Patriarch would command the Jerusalem garrison. As knights of the realm, the Knights of the Holy Sepulchre would marry and assume feudal responsibilities. This was a unique characteristic of the Order and set it apart from the other military orders established later on. The Canons formed a second tier of the Order, and were invested by the Latin Patriarch. They would remain celibate, would contribute to martial actions, and lived according to the Augustinian disciplines. Canonesses formed a third tier of the Order, performed charitable works, and were also celibate and lived religious lives.

The Knights were key to sustaining the Kingdom of Jerusalem. Upon the initial conquest, the great majority of the crusaders returned to their realms in Europe. The Knight protectors of the Holy Sepulchre stayed with their lord, Godfrey, and maintained the constant warfare on the realm's perimeter. This gave the Kingdom an initial year to form. Upon Godfrey's death, the bold Tancred of the famous de Hauteville lineage, attempted to seize the throne, since with it came the overlordship of all Crusader states, collectively called Outrehmer. Godfrey's faithful vassal, Warner of Gray, occupied the Tower of David, manning it with Godfrey's personal guard, undoubtedly drawn from the Knights of the Holy Sepulchre. He dispatched Robert, Bishop of Ramleh with two protector knights north to Edessa to alert Godfrey's brother Baldwin of his brother's death and invite him to claim the throne. This was critical in so much as Baldwin proved to be superior in his later consolidation of resources and maintenance of the Kingdom. Baldwin's harrowing march southward is the text of legend and exemplified his strength of faith and courage so needed for overlordship of the Crusader states and leadership of the Knights of the Holy Sepulchre. Baldwin accepted the title of King, thus beginning the century of the Crusader Kingdom of Jerusalem. The century was marked by a heroic struggle to hold out against the surrounding Muslim states and the animosity of the

*"The Road to Jerusalem"*

Gustav Doré (1832–1883) from *The History of the Crusades*
by Joseph François Michaud (1767–1839)

Byzantine emperor.

In 1137, Emperor John of Comenius made the first territorial encroachment by capturing the Christian city of Antioch. This began the disintegration of the Crusader Holy Land. On July 4, 1187, Saladin with his infidel horde, having united the Muslim religion against Christianity, met the Christian defenders of the Holy Land on the shore of Lake Tiberias and completely annihilated them. Advised by the Templars, King Guy of Jerusalem had decided on a forced march across a water-less area in the middle of summer. The battle force of the Crusaders found them-selves caught in a trap between the hills known as the Horns of Hattin and the Sea of Galilee. The Crusader forces, parched with thirst and sweltering in their heavy armor, were unable to escape from the Saracen light calvary and were slaughtered almost to the last man. The way became open for the Muslims to capture nearly every one of the ports of the Mediterranean on which the Crusaders had to rely for their reinforcements and supplies. Later that year in October, the Saracen leader Saladin succeeded in recapturing Jerusalem. Saladin granted safe conduct to the Knights of the Holy Sepulchre, who together with the Knights of the other orders, retreated to the various castles and strongholds from whence constant battles continued.

The Latin Kingdom did not fall with Jerusalem and was reestablished at St. John of Acre through the leadership of Richard the Lionheart. It was in 1191 that the Port of St. John of Acre was retaken. This was to be a vital base from which the Knights were able to continue the struggle for another hundred years and from which they were able to evacuate the remains of the Christian forces.

On February 20, 1229, Frederick II, the Emperor of the Holy Roman Empire, concluded a treaty with the Sultan an-Nasir who agreed to restore Jerusalem to the Christians on condition that the Muslims should be free to practice their religion in the mosque of Omar. The Emperor proclaimed himself King of Jerusalem and the Crusaders returned to the city. The terms of the treaty were met with indignation by the Christians in Jerusalem who were not prepared to accept coexistence with the Muslims. Frederick II thereupon gave up all interest in the Holy Land which he abandoned. This represented a final chance for Outremer to consolidate its strength, but it failed. Consequently, Jerusalem passed from the hands of the Crusaders for the final time in 1244. They withdrew to Acre as their last stronghold while the Khwarismian horsemen devastated the Holy Sepulchre and the tomb of Godfrey de Bouillon.

The Latin Kingdom in St. John of Acre endured numerous Mohammedan onslaughts until 1291 when the fortified city capitulated to Sultan Malek-Ascharf after a fierce battle. According to tradition, during the last siege the Patriarch of Jerusalem, Nicholas de Hannapes, gathered around him a body of his Knights of the Holy Sepulchre to hold one of the main bastions, Fort Montreal, which was captured by the Saracens only after the defenders had all perished.

# CHAPTER 4

# DEVELOPMENTS IN EUROPE

After the loss of the Holy Land, the Knights of the Holy Sepulchre, animated still by the spirit of faith and devotion, gathered together in different countries. They either joined existing priories or founded new ones. There was an early priory in Warwick, England where Canons of the Order under Henry de Newburg founded it during the reign of King Henry I in the beginning of the twelfth century. The Church of St. Mary in Warwick is built on the site of this priory where the original crypt still exists. In 1174, King Henry II initiated the construction of the Church of the Holy Sepulchre in Cambridge and the one in Northampton both of which survived the suppression of monasteries and priories under Henry VIII.

At that time, other priories existed in Ireland, Scotland, Italy, Poland, France, Sicily, Cyprus, Germany, Holland, and Sweden. These consisted of monasteries of canons and convents of canonesses. There were some two thousand of these priories spread all over Europe. The acknowledged head of the priories was an Archpriory in Perugia, Italy. The Priors of Perugia bore the title of Grand Priors of the Order. The titular Patriarch of Jerusalem no longer exercised any jurisdiction.

The Knights of the Holy Sepulchre received many donations of land and money in Europe to assist them in their defense of the Christian shrines. The most spectacular of these donations was in the last will and testament of King Alfonso I who died in 1134. He named as his heirs and successors in the Kingdom of Aragon and Navarre the Orders of the Holy Sepulchre, the Hospitallers, and the Templars who equally shared his whole kingdom. The three orders did not pursue their claims resulting in Ramiro II, brother of Alfonso, assuming the throne. However, all three of the Orders were amply compensated by Ramiro with grants of land and fortresses in Aragon and Catalonia.

During the Fifth Crusade led by the Kings of Hungary and Cyprus, a small contingent of Hungarian knights were "almost annihilated in a snowstorm" in an attempt to cross the Lebanon. Among the few survivors of that winter of 1217-1218 were a handful who had received the accolade of Knighthood at the Holy Sepulchre and later formed a priory in Hungary. This gave the Hungarians claim to the oldest continuous establishment of the Order in Central Europe. Their priory lasted until World War II at which time it became inactive. After the war the communists suppressed it into physical extinction.

Prince Jaksa Grye of Miechow sponsored Sir Martin Gall and other Knights of the Holy Sepulchre. He imported several sacks of soil from the Tomb of the Holy

Sepulchre in Jerusalem. A wooden church was first built, followed by a stone abbey replete with the replica of Christ's tomb. Additionally, a Polish nobleman, Henry of Sansomir, with some of his peers who had returned from a year in the Holy Land, established a priory of the Order at Perugia. This priory passed from Perugia to the Grand Prior of Meichow in Poland. It survived until 1818, when that part of Poland was incorporated into the Russian Empire and Czar Alexander I abolished all Catholic monasteries and convents.

The Holy Land was still the heart of the Order, however, and efforts continued to develop a Christian presence there. In 1333, Robert of Anjou, King of the Two Sicilies, gained a limited access to Jerusalem and the Holy Places for Christians by paying a huge ransom to the Sultan of Egypt. After this, the period of pilgrimages was renewed, and the Muslims discovered that the pilgrim trade could be lucrative and did not discourage it.

By the middle of the fifteenth century, many of the military orders founded in Palestine were in eclipse because they no longer had territorial bases in the East from which to fight the infidel. However, the Order of the Hospitallers of St. John was at the time firmly established on the Island of Rhodes. Because activities of the other orders were necessarily restricted, Pope Pius II considered joining them together in a single military force under the patronage of the Blessed Virgin and giving them headquarters on the Island of Lemnos from which to continue their fight against the Muslims. The project was abandoned because of opposition from the orders and due to the loss of Lemnos to the Turks. In 1489, Pope Innocent VIII considered suppressing the Orders of the Holy Sepulchre and St. Lazare in order to unite them and their property to the Knights of Rhodes (Malta) who had already been given the wealth of the Templars on their suppression. The Pope's intention was in this way to combine all the forces of Christendom in the fight against the Turks. Again, there was immediate opposition from the orders and in addition from powerful rulers including the Holy Roman Emperor and the kings of France, Sicily, and Aragon. The plan was no more successful than that of Pius II.

The reconquest of Spain from the Moors with considerable assistance from the Knights of the Holy Sepulchre in 1492 was successful. In the same year, Alexander VI became Pope. He was of Spanish origin and at once put a stop to the execution of the edict of his predecessors in order not to sow discord among the orders of chivalry when union against the Turkish menace was more than ever necessary. In a bull of 1496, he confirmed the continued independent existence of the Order of the Holy Sepulchre, *reserved to the Supreme Pontiff the title of Grand Master*, and confirmed to the Franciscan custodian of the Holy Land the right of investing new knights and renewed the old conditions that had to be fulfilled by each candidate.

Undaunted in their hopes of taking over the other orders, the Knights of Rhodes obtained from Pope Julius II in 1505, a new edict reaffirming that of Innocent VIII in respect to their acquiring the properties of the other orders situated in Western Europe. Yet the edict was to maintain the independence and the privileges of the Order of the Holy Sepulchre in Eastern Europe. Additionally, the Pope made a treaty with Venice requiring that the Venetians provide fifty ships to the Knights of Rhodes for a new Crusade against the Turks. The necessity of equipping this fleet made it necessary for the Knights of Rhodes to press for the reimplementation of the Edict of Innocent VIII. To maintain peace between Venice, Bohemia, and Hungary, Julius II reassured the Grand Prior at Miechow that there would be no interference with the Knights and privileges of the Order of the Holy Sepulchre in the East. However, the Order of the Holy Sepulchre continued to flourish independently in Flanders, France, Germany, Spain, and elsewhere. The period of official, yet not factual, amalgamation of the Order ended when Pope Leo X in 1513 and 1517 definitely and finally rescinded the Edict of Innocent VIII, yielding to the entreaty of Ferdinand, the Catholic King of Aragon. This freed the Order of the Holy Sepulchre from any obedience to the Order of Rhodes (Malta). The Order of the Holy Sepulchre continued its uninterrupted existence with investiture of candidates continuing to take place in the Basilica of the Holy Sepulchre, thus maintaining the Order's essential association with Jerusalem.

# CHAPTER 5

# THE ORDER FROM THE SIXTEENTH CENTURY THROUGH THE NINETEENTH CENTURY

In the middle of the sixteenth century, the naval situation in the Mediterranean Sea was the cause of considerable anxiety. Christian ships were constantly being attacked, captured, or sunk by the Turks who controlled the sea. A meeting of Priors and Knights of the Holy Sepulchre was held at Hoogestraten in the Netherlands on March 26, 1558, for the purpose of gathering together all the Christian Naval Forces to destroy the Turkish fleet and to liberate the Mediterranean. The priors and knights at the meeting elected Philip II, King of Spain, later of Armada fame, Grand Master of the Order. The Knights believed that Philip was the only man capable of leading an international fleet. By placing under his authority the properties and priories of the Order, they knew it would be easier to obtain loans necessary for the project.

In 1559, Philip II, living at that time in Brussels, left for Spain. To pay for the expedition against the Turks, he ordered a special minting of gold coins bearing the arms of the Order of the Holy Sepulchre. Thereafter, the Duke of Medina, Celi, assumed command and assembled the galleons of the different Italian States and those of Malta. With ten thousand men, the fleet sailed from Syracuse in December 1559. Being delayed by contrary winds, the Turkish fleet was able to intercept them resulting in a disastrous defeat with heavy losses in the battle of Djerba. Six years later, the Turkish fleet was checked by the heroic defense of Malta by the Sovereign Order of St. John of Jerusalem. Then in 1571, Pope Pius V organized the Christian defense under Don John of Austria. An allied fleet was assembled that defeated the Turks at the battle of LePanto in 1571. This victory temporarily ended Ottoman domination of the Mediterranian Sea, the Ionian Sea, and the Gulf of Corinth.

Being aware of the responsibilities and remembering how similar commitments had affected the strength of his father, Charles V, Philip II felt it necessary to resign the office of Grand Master of the Order of the Holy Sepulchre. Later in 1615, the French Duc de Nevers attempted to become Grand Master but was unsuccessful due to a delegation from the Order of St. John persuading King Louis XIII to stop his efforts.

Succeeding Grand Masters were Philip III, King of Spain, 1598; Philip IV, King of Spain, 1621; and Charles II, King of Spain, 1667. The failure of the unification of the Order under a royal temporal protector indicated that the Knights of the Holy Sepulchre wanted no union other than their spiritual alliance with the Holy Land. Desirous to reside close to their priories in their own countries, they looked for protection to their own Kings or Princes with the recognition of only one Grand Master, the Guardian of the Franciscan Custody, representing the Sovereign Pontiff.

Finally, Benedict XIV in "Supremo Militantis Ecclesiae" dated January 17, 1795, revised the Rules of the Order. The forms by which the Franciscan Custodian should be guided in bestowing insignia were fixed, and the Knights were granted the right to use the title "Count of the Sacred Palace of the Lateran."

At the beginning of the nineteenth century, the Order had neither unity of purpose nor prescribed duty that had been sought for centuries. It had lost churches, houses, priories, and protection. Only memories remained of the glorious past. There were moments of discomfort and bewilderment in this century of reforms and battles. The French Revolution had made all of Europe tremble, transformed institutions, and destroyed centuries-old customs. It had serious repercussions on the Order, although of a less serious extent than on other Orders, some of which disappeared forever, swept away in the tempestuous floods of the Revolution. Illustrious Orders, such as that of Malta, were forced to go into exile, losing the prestige that they had for centuries. The Order of the Holy Sepulchre reorganized itself, seeking help from various sources who still cherished the Cross of Jerusalem.

To strengthen the Knights it was necessary to unite them under the command of an authoritative Grand Master. Thus it was that Pius IX on December 10, 1847, reestablished the Patriarchate of Jerusalem and placed the Order under the Patriarch. Pius IX decreed "with all the rights that have been carefully studied remaining in force, it is decreed that the conferring of rank in the Order of the Holy Sepulchre shall belong exclusively to the Patriarch. He shall, however, use this privilege *only in favor of those who have been worthy in the cause of religion and who manifest other requirements for obtaining this honor.*" The Order was then able to have Lieutenancies and Knights who were to be governed by a single rule throughout the world.

Pius IX entrusted the bestowing of Knighthood of the Holy Sepulchre once again to the Latin Patriarch. The Pope appointed the Most Reverend Joseph Valerga, an expert on the Middle East and its languages, as the first Latin Patriarch of Jerusalem of the modern period. As soon as he took possession of the Patriarchate in January 1848, he was invested in the Order by the guardian of the Holy Land and immediately assumed the duty of Grand Master. To satisfy Patriarch Valerga, Pius IX granted "for the greater splendor and increase" of the Order, three distinctive ranks in the Order: Grand Cross, Commander, and Knight insignia. The single rank that existed since the time of the Crusades did not adequately reward diverse merits. Also the form of the decoration and character of the military uniform was established.

As an intermediary between himself and the Holy See, the Patriarch appointed a Delegate of the Order. The first was Count Gaetano Agnelli di Malherbe of Urbino. After Count Agnelli's death, Count Fani, personal chamberlain to Pope Pius IX, was appointed. The Count's jurisdiction extended over the whole Pontifical State, including Tuscany. Thus, the Order was reestablished in Tuscany at Florence in 1850.

On August 3, 1888, Pope Leo XIII, by an apostolic letter, extended the honor of the Order to women, an obvious innovation. It represented a return to a former tradition when, in the seventeenth century and earlier, the canonesses of the Holy Sepulchre were at the heart of the Order. Moreover, women had indeed been knighted during the medieval period for their acts of military valor under exigent situations such as at Tortosa in 1149. Consequently, the election of women constituted the ideal continuation of a former tradition. Women so honored were to be styled Dames of the Holy Sepulchre (called Ladies in English speaking nations) and were to share in all of the rights and privileges of the Knights. They were entitled to wear a black cloak with the insignia of the Order, the Jerusalem Cross in red.

Lady Mary Lomax, an English countess, was one of the first women admitted into the Order in the modern period. This took place on April 15, 1871. In a publication in Paris in 1849, by Eugene DeRosier, there are listed the names of several noble Ladies who had in the past belonged to the Order. However, the tradition had fallen into disuse before the beginning of the fifteenth century. From 1873 to 1889, the number of Ladies was about one hundred. Since that time, the number has increased significantly, and the Ladies now execute a major role in the Order, both in Europe and the United States of America.

By the end of the nineteenth century, the Order had embarked upon an era of growth and expansion, and it numbered about two thousand persons. Among its confreres were the King of Spain, the Emperor and Empress of Austria, and many leading noblemen of Europe including confreres of the royal houses of Belgium, Portugal, Italy, Luxembourg, and the Duke of Norfolk in England.

# CHAPTER 6

# THE ORDER IN THE TWENTIETH CENTURY

A major reform of the Order occurred in May 1907, when Pope Pius X issued a bull that changed some aspects of externalisms and administration. By this decree a number of changes were made in the conduct and makeup of the Order. They included:

- Permission to wear the Cross of the Order suspended from a military trophy
- Reservation of the office of Grand Master and Protector of the Order to show its military origin for himself
- Fixing the number of classes of Knights and Dames (Ladies) at four
- Approve the creation of chapters, called Lieutenancies, in each country in which the Order existed
- Empowering Lieutenants to enroll proper and eligible persons in the Order making it unnecessary for the candidate to travel to Jerusalem to be invested
- Prescribed a uniform of white and gold for Knights (which Pope Paul VI later rescinded)
- Appointment of the Patriarch of Jerusalem as his Lieutenant and administrator of the Order

Pope Pius X entrusted to the Order the work of the preservation and propagation of the Faith in Palestine. He encouraged assistance to and development of the missions of the Latin Patriarchate of Jerusalem, providing for its charitable and social undertaking and the defense of the rights of the Catholic Church in the Holy Land, the cradle of the Order. He exhorted the Knights to revive in modern form the spirit and ideals of the Crusades with the weapons of the Faith, that is, apostolic and Christian charity. It was at this time that a fourth class of Knights and Ladies was created, the rank of Knight or Lady with Plaque (Star). This was to be given for "special merit" and named such Grand Officers senior in precedence to Commander but junior to Knight Grand Cross.

Pope Pius X continued to hold the office of Grand Master until his death in 1914. In 1928, Pope Pius XI reappointed the Patriarch of Jerusalem "Rector Et Administrator" of the Order. During the same year the Pope, recognizing the need to strengthen the Faith in the Holy Land, attached "Association for the Preservation of the Faith in Palestine" to the Order.

In 1930, a serious controversy arose between the Sovereign Military Order of Malta and the Equestrian Order of the Holy Sepulchre of Jerusalem over certain questions of protocol. A commission of cardinals was formed by Pope Pius XI to consider the problem. The findings promulgated on September 1, 1931, include among others that the Order could not use "sacred" or "military" in their title but to use instead the word "Equestrian".

On March 19, 1932, a new constitution was approved by Pope Pius XI, clarifying the organizational structure of the Order and the duties of the "Bailif" or Lieutenant in each national Lieutenancy.

The first worldwide Congress of the Order was held in Jerusalem on September 6 to 14, 1932, with His Beatitude, Patriarch Barlissini, presiding. This was the forerunner of meetings called "Consultas," now held every four years in Rome. Delegations were present from Austria, Belgium, Czechoslovakia, France, Germany, Italy, England, Spain, Hungary, Canada, Portugal, Mexico, and the United States, testifying to the international character of the Order.

Foreseeing the outbreak of World War II, the Patriarch Barlissini asked the Holy Father that a Roman prelate be designated to take charge of the interests of the Order during the conflict. In a brief of Pope Pius XII of June 16, 1940, he nominated Nicolo Cardinal Canali as Protector of the Order.

In a *Motu Proprio* of August 15, 1945, the Pope assigned the Church and Monastery of St. Onofrio on the Janiculum Hill in Rome to be the new headquarters of the Order and mother church. Devotion to St. Onofrio, a holy hermit who lived in Egypt in the early years of Christianity, was brought back to Europe by returning Crusaders. The Pope chose this property partly because of its association with the poet Torquato Tasso, who in the adjoining cloister had composed a number of his beautiful poems about the Holy Land and the Crusaders, but mainly because of its location near Vatican City. The Church contains the tomb of Tasso, considered the greatest Italian poet after Dante Alighieri.

In addition, the Order restored a palace on the Via della Conciliazione close to the Basilica of St. Peter's, for use as offices, the consulta, and official receptions. It is now used as the international headquarters of the Order. A part of the palace was developed as the Hotel Columbus to provide an income for the Grand Magisterium to meet its administration expenses.

Beginning in 1948, the Order commenced to be awakened from its lethargic slumber caused by the devastations wrought by the successive deprivations of World War I, the Great Depression, and World War II. This awakening was engineered through the efforts of Msgr. Abraham D'Assemani, an Arab. Although he stimulated interest in the Middle East, Italy, and Spain, his greatest efforts were here in the USA. Specifically, he was aided by Cardinal Dougherty, Archbishop of Philadelphia, and by a fine Catholic layman, Michael Francis Doyle of Philadelphia. Subsequently, Bishop Francis Spellman, later Cardinal, became a dominant proponent of the Order in America.

With the situation in Palestine, Pope Pius XII issued the Apostolic Brief "Quam

Romani Pontificis" on September 14, 1949, promulgating new statutes of the Order. It abolished the mandate "Association for the Preservation of the Faith in Palestine" and gave the Order a special mission for the first time since the Age of the Crusaders:

> The preservation and the propagation of the faith in Palestine, assistance to and development of the mission of the Latin Patriarchate of Jerusalem, providing for its charitable, cultural, and social undertakings, and the defense of the rights of the Catholic Church in the Holy Land, the cradle of the Order.

The Apostolic Brief constituted the Order as a "juridical person," an organized entity having a single legal identity. The Brief created the Office of Cardinal Grand Master, vested in Cardinal Canali, and designated the Latin Patriarchate of Jerusalem as the Grand Prior of the entire Order. Among other provisions, the new statutes (Constitution) provided for Knights and Ladies of the Collar, limited to twelve in memory of the twelve Apostles, to honor Knights and Ladies of high dignity and exceptional character. Two decorations were instituted: the Palm of Jerusalem and the Cross of Merit to be conferred upon persons of high merit for services to the Church and the Order. A special insignia, the Pilgrim's Shell, was authorized and designed for Knights and Ladies of the Order making a pilgrimage to the Holy Land.

Cardinal Canali died in 1961, and Eugene Cardinal Tisserant was appointed his successor. At the same time Pope John XXIII approved a revised Constitution for the Order by the Apostolic Letter "Religiossimo Monumento Victoriae" on December 8, 1962, in which the Order's juridical status was confirmed and the protection of the Holy See reconfirmed. Since that date on the Feast of the Immaculate Conception, the Order has been under the personal protection of the Holy Father. Thus, it is part of the Holy See.

The provisions of the revised Constitution in 1962 were reinforced in the revision of November 19, 1967, by Pope Paul VI. In them, the Holy See acts as the Protector of the Order while its government is in the hands of a Cardinal Grand Master appointed by the Supreme Pontiff. The power to create Knights and Ladies is given to the Cardinal Grand Master who obtains the Seal of the Secretariat of State from His Holiness for each creation. The Patriarch of Jerusalem becomes the Grand Prior of the Order and retains a limited power to nominate Knights and Ladies with such nominations approved by the Cardinal Grand Master. Rome is designated the seat of the Order while its historical site remains at Jerusalem.

Upon the death of Cardinal Tisserant in 1973, Cardinal Maximilian de Furstenberg became Grand Master. Under his authority, Pope Paul VI approved further new statutes in 1977. Under Maximilian Cardinal de Furstenberg there was a considerable expansion of the Order. Upon his death in 1987, Pope John Paul II designated Joseph Cardinal Caprio as his successor, followed in 1996 by Carlo Cardinal Furno.

# CHAPTER 7

# THE LATIN PATRIARCHATE OF JERUSALEM

The first Bishop of Jerusalem was St. James The Less, son of Alphaeus. His life was so pure and so beautiful that he was called "The Just." Thrown from the summit of the Temple, he died praying for his executioners. His martyrdom occurred between 35 and 65A.D. His successor (61–107 A.D.), St. Simon, was crucified when he was 120 years old. Some of the dire events of those days, foretold by Our Lord, include: the siege, capture, and sacking of Jerusalem under Vespasian and Titus; vengeance of the Romans on the rebellious Jews; and the taking of the city once more and its destruction by Hadrian thereafter calling it Aelia Capitolina.

Other bishops of Jerusalem were: St. Jude, martyred in 135; St. Mark, martyred in 156; St. Narcissus in 202; St. Alexander, martyred in 249; and St. Zambdas in 302. Peace and tranquility followed due to Emperor Constantine the Great. From 313 to 333 Marcarius was Bishop of Jerusalem, followed by St. Maximus (334–349), St. Cyril (350–386), and St. John (389–415).

One should not forget Julian the Apostate who failed to raise the Temple from its ruins nor St. Jerome in the fifth century. In 418, with Juvenal (422–458), the Bishop of Jerusalem took the title of Patriarch because of the exceptional glories and importance of the See of Jerusalem. The title of Patriarch was recognized and approved by civil and ecclesiastical authorities. From Julian to the coming of the Crusaders, Jerusalem had eighty-eight bishops.

*His Beatitude, Michel Sabbah,*
*Latin Patriarch of Jerusalem,*
*Grand Prior, Knight of the Collar*

Between 418 and 1099, great misfortunes harassed the Holy City and its inhabitants: invasion by the Persians with Chosroes; the invasion under the Caliph Omar; and the fierce persecution of the Caliph Hakim who, at the beginning of the tenth century, burned alive the Patriarch Orestes, his own kinsman. In 1099, when the Crusaders conquered Jerusalem, they found the Patriarchal See vacant on account of the death of its incumbent, the Patriarch Simeon of the Syrian rite. The Crusaders, in keeping with the custom of the time, replaced him with a Patriarch of their own rite—the Latin Rite. Arnold [Arnulf], who was made the Patriarch, was deposed the same year. Dogbert [Dagobert], the Papal Legate, then became Patriarch, and ruled over Palestine until 1107. His successors were:

| | |
|---|---|
| Gibelin | 1107–1112 |
| Arnold (for the second time ) | 1112–1116 |
| Guarimus | 1118–1128 |
| Stephen | 1128–1130 |
| William I | 1130–1144 |
| Fulcher | 1147–1157 |
| Amauri | 1157–1180 |
| Heraclius | 1180–1191 |
| Albert I The Hermit (nephew of Peter the Hermit) | 1191–1194 |
| Monaco | 1194–1203 |
| Godfrey | 1203–1204 |
| Albert II | 1204–1214 |
| Rudolph | 1214–1216 |
| Lotharius | 1216–1224 |

All retained the same authority until 1369, even after the fall of Acre in 1291, though the Patriarch did not reside in Palestine. From 1369 until 1847, the Franciscans possessed and exercised jurisdiction with untold suffering and sometimes death.

It was only in 1847 that Pope Pius IX reestablished the Hierarchy with a resident Latin Patriarch in Jerusalem. The first resident Latin Patriarch was Archbishop Joseph Valerga, former missionary to the Middle East, chosen when only thirty-four years of age. On October 10, 1847, the Pope in person bestowed the episcopal consecration and the pallium on the new Patriarch. Having taken possession of his See, the newly appointed Patriarch gave himself wholeheartedly to developing the works of charity and education already undertaken so meritoriously and successfully by the Custos of the Holy Land.

Carrying out, without delay, his apostolic plans, Patriarch Valerga introduced the Sisters of the Apparition from France. They immediately opened the first school for girls; two years later in 1850 the first hospital; in 1852 the first school for girls in Bethlehem; and in 1856, the first orphanage. In 1855 he obtained the services of the Sisters of Notre Dame de Nazareth who opened a school, an orphanage, and a dispensary in Nazareth. They opened a school and a dispensary in Haifa at St. John of Acre, at Shefa Amic, and elsewhere. He encouraged the foundation in 1880 of the Sisters of the Rosary for native Sisters only. Since their foundation, they have rendered valuable services to the Patriarchate in the villages of Palestine.

For the training of a diocesan clergy, Patriarch Valerga, in the first year of his episcopacy, found ten native recruits in the Franciscan parishes. Not having a seminary, he sent them to the seminary the Jesuits had opened in Lebanon at Ghazia. In 1852, he opened his own seminary in Jerusalem and, in the following year, raised a building at Beit Jala to house his seminarians. This building already imposing for those days, was enlarged by two wings in 1957–1959 and is still the established seminary at the present time.

Patriarch Valerga, through a response to his appeal to a number of priests in France and Italy, was able to start the first parish and country schools: at Beit Jala in 1853; at Gifnan in 1856; at Ramallah in 1857; at Bir-Zeit in 1858; at Beit Sahour in 1859; in Taybeh in 1860; and at Salt IV Transjordan in 1866. The last mission was the first Catholic parish of any rite to be opened across the Jordan River since the Crusaders' times, marking the reentrance of Catholicism in Transjordan. In 1863, Patriarch Valerga encouraged the construction of a hospice for pilgrims in Jerusalem, the first after that of the Casa Nova of the Franciscans—the Austrian Hospice.

Patriarch Valerga was charged with the Apostolic Delegation of Aleppo and Syria, which he visited regularly. In fact, his untimely death on December 1, 1871, after four days illness, was caused by the water he drank while visiting the Bedouins. In an echo of the crusader past, he suffered the same manner of demise visited upon Godfrey de Bouillon. The Patriarch was buried in the Procathedral of the Most Holy Name of Jesus of the Patriarchate, since the Cathedral of the Patriarch is officially the Holy Sepulchre. He organized and governed the Archdiocese for twenty-four years, leaving a sound foundation of Catholicism in the Holy Land.

The successor to Patriarch Valerga was Patriarch Vincent Bracco, who zealously and wholeheartedly strove to propagate the Kingdom of God so as to restore all of Palestine to Christ. During the sixteen years of his rule, he continued and developed the work already begun by his predecessor. He opened twelve new missions, sending his missionaries beyond the Jordan to the plateau of Moab and Galaad, to the tents of the Bedouins. His health, never strong, ended with his death of pneumonia in June 1889. Pope Leo XIII on the news of his death said "the Church of Jerusalem has just lost a treasure."

The third Latin Patriarch of Jerusalem was Patriarch Ludovic Piavi, O.F.M., who died in 1905. His general ability was recognized as he worked hard to gain a mastery of the Arabic language. He served as Apostolic Delegate to Syria in 1875, prior to his appointment as Latin Patriarch of Jerusalem in 1889.

On the death of Patriarch Piavi, the Patriarchate was placed on the shoulders of Archbishop Philip Maris Camassei, greatly appreciated for his gentility and humility. Patriarch Camassei raised the already high standard of the course of studies of the Latin Seminary by directing the teaching of Latin, Greek, Turkish, French, Italian, and Arabic. With the beginning of World War I, Turkey unfurled the banner of her prophet and declared a Holy War. Because of Muslim fanaticism, the Patriarch was exiled to Nazareth. A reign of terror ensued. Religious houses were seized by the government, Church property destroyed, and the Holy Vessels confiscated. Muslim rule ended when, on December 1, 1917, General Allenby, head of the British force, entered Jerusalem on foot through the Damascus Gate, followed by the Commanders of the French and Italian detachments, heads of political missions, and military attachés.

Patriarch Camassei was released from Turkish captivity and reentered Jerusalem in great triumph. He immediately set out to visit the missions, to gather the scattered flock, and to begin the work of reconstruction. His delicate health had been exhausted by ill treatment, and he died in 1921, after his elevation to the Cardinalate.

The Order remained dormant from 1914 to 1918 due to the shocking deprivations of World War I. During the next ten years, recovery from the war's aftermath was on the horizon. Suddenly the world was in the upwind of the colossal depression of 1929 to 1935. When the economic distress was fading, the horrors of World War II commenced in 1939, lasting until 1945.

Patriarch Louis Barlassina governed the Archdiocese with zest and courage from 1921 to 1947, during the British Mandate. During his patriarchate, subsequent to 1940, the Latin Patriarch of Jerusalem became the Grand Prior of the Order. His Beatitude Barlassina died on September 21, 1947, on the eve of the partition of Palestine, which was decided by the United Nations on November 29, 1947. A year later in 1948, the sad Israeli-Arab War followed. Archbishop Gori became the next Latin Patriarch.

Prior to 1948, all the territory of the Archdioceses of Jerusalem (Palestine, Jordan and Cyprus) were under the authority of Great Britain. After 1948, the area of the Archdiocese was divided into four political sectors that could not communicate with one another and were subject to governments that were hostile to one another. One part of Palestine became the State of Israel; the Gaza Strip was under Egyptian control; the West Bank and Transjordan constituted the Hashemite Kingdom of Jordan; and Cyprus remained under British control until it obtained its independence in 1960.

Due to the 1948 War, several parishes and Catholic institutions disappeared completely or became mere shadows of what they had been. In Transjordan, the sudden presence of thousands of refugees brought about serious problems of reorganization in schools, churches, and social institutions. From day to day, communications between the different sectors of the Archdiocese became more and more difficult. At the same time there was a sad exodus to the United States, Canada, Australia, and other countries, of numerous native-born Christians. Patriarch Gori died in 1970, extremely saddened by the turn of events over which he had no control. He did everything possible to continue the activities of the Patriarchate. The 1967 War did not help matters as communication between Jerusalem and Transjordan became more difficult. The emigration of Christians increased. The morale of the population sank further as Palestinians could not see any hope of finding a peaceful solution to the worsening conditions of native Christians.

This was the situation confronting His Beatitude James Joseph Beltritti, who succeeded Patriarch Gori after serving as chancellor and then coadjutor to the Patriarch. In this state of uncertainty, the Patriarchate, the Custody, and Catholic communities of the Holy Land continued, as much as possible, their welfare activities. Patriarch Beltritti, undaunted, went on with his work greatly encouraged by the support, financial and prayerful, of the Knights and Ladies of the Holy Sepulchre of Jerusalem, the Order having prospered greatly during this period. Patriarch Beltritti retired in January 1988 and was succeeded by His Beatitude Michel Sabbah, the first Palestinian Christian to be so chosen.

Serious problems continue to plague the new Patriarch—the refugee situation with over two million living in refugee camps in miserable conditions, continuing expulsion of Palestinians, and the Palestinian uprising, called the Intifada begun in 1987. Moreover, Christians in the Holy Land are constantly emigrating for economic, social, or political reasons: economic, to find better means elsewhere; social, to escape the anti-Christian pressure; and political, to gain a say in their own destinies. Patriarch Sabbah is endeavoring to stem the tide of emigration and is seeking aid from the Order and other organizations of the Catholic Church. The help needed now includes:

- Support of families that have lost income
- Rebuilding houses that have been destroyed
- Aid to families whose properties have been plundered
- Clothing for prisoners

Additional Catholic organizations that have contributed significant aid include the Catholic Near East Welfare Association and the Pontifical Mission for Palestine. Patriarch Sabbah said this is very much appreciated as they are made to feel protected and supported in their difficulties. Yet in this state of uncertainty, the Latin Patriarchate, the Custody, and the Catholic Communities continue as much as possible their endeavors to preserve the Christian presence and to normalize their existence.

The Holy Land, from a religious point of view, has always been a composite country. In the Old Testament times, side by side with the worship of Yahweh, there were the religions of the Canaanites and that of other ancestries; in the early Christian era from the first to the seventh century, Jews, Samaritans, Pagans; from the seventh to the eleventh centuries, Christians, Jews, Samaritans, and Moslems; and from the eleventh century to the present, Jews, Christians, Moslems, a few Samaritans, and a minority of Druze. The table shows the situation in 1990:

| | Israel | West Bank & Gaza | Jordan | Cyprus | Total |
|---|---|---|---|---|---|
| Jews | 3,659,000 | 70,000 | | | 3,729,000 |
| Moslems | 634,600 | 1,364,000 | 2,666,100 | 140,000 | 4,804,700 |
| Christians | 105,000 | 50,000 | 130,000 | 611,400 | 896,400 |
| | 4,398,600 | 1,484,000 | 2,796,100 | 751,400 | 9,430,100 |
| Area (sq. miles) | 16,320 | 2,379 | 35,000 | 3,572 | 57,271 |

Christians are to be found in Jordan, Galilee, the West Bank, and in and around Jerusalem (Jerusalem, Nazareth, Bethlehem, Ramallah). In Palestine as well as Jordan and Gaza they constitute only a minority. Approximately half of the Catholics are of the Latin Rite. In 1990, the work of the Latin Patriarchate encompassed the following:

**Catholics of the Latin Rite:** approximately 55,000, including Cyprus

**Parishes:** 55, of which 14 are administered by the Franciscan Fathers, one by the Carmelite Fathers, and 40 by diocesan clergy

**Religious:** 431, including 179 brothers and 252 priests belonging to 16 different Orders or Congregations, the majority of which are foreigners and are not engaged in specific pastoral works

**Nuns:** 1164 belonging to 30 different Congregations, of which 94 are assigned to schools

**Diocesan Seminary:** 88 seminarians, all native-born

**Schools:** 90 with 40,000 pupils, of which 14,878 attend 42 parish schools of the Patriarchate

**Lay teachers and Service Personnel of Parish Schools:** 699

**Welfare Institutions:**
    Hospitals and Maternities – 10
    Orphanages – 7
    Dispensaries – 20
    Old People's Homes – 7
    Schools for the Deaf – 2

In addition, mention should be made of the schools and institutions belonging to other Catholic Churches of the Eastern Tradition, the Pontifical Mission for Palestine established in 1948 for the Palestinian refugees, and the Catholic Relief Services of the Episcopal Conference of the United States. The two Caritas hospitals of Jerusalem and Jordan founded after the 1967 War and the Baby's Hospital established in Bethlehem by the Swiss and German Caritas were made possible by the Order of the Holy Sepulchre. This, indeed, is an impressive work carried out by the Catholic Church in the Holy Land.

The current events in the Holy Land are a great challenge to Christians in ensuring the Christian presence there. Knights and Ladies of the Equestrian Order of the Holy Sepulchre of Jerusalem realize the need to take on ever-widening roles in the work of the Latin Patriarchate to fulfill the objective of the Order. As a result, they are responding to the challenge with loyalty and dedication to their special vocation for the Holy Land. Education is among the principal needs of the Christian community, for unless the Church continues to educate Christians at all levels, the future would be bleak. Without schools, Christian children, already living in a non-Christian milieu, would be obliged to attend public schools where the atmosphere and mentality are contrary to Christianity. At these schools no Christian thought or culture is allowed. It is heartening to know that the Catholic Church school system is equal to and in many cases superior to the public system. Their high standards must be maintained and require increased support to meet escalating expenses.

The educational needs of the Christian community do not cease with primary and secondary schools. A crying need for both Christians and Moslems lies in university training. Realizing this, Pope Paul VI initiated Bethlehem University with the support of the Order. In contrast, the Hebrew University, which is internationally known, has an enrollment of approximately 20,000 students of which less than 200 are Arabs. Bethlehem University has two thousand students, 60% of whom are Muslims.

Closely entwined with educational needs of Christians in the Holy Land are their economic needs. The majority of the people are lower middle-class. There is a fair-sized middle-class and only a few who are wealthy. In general all three classes derive their livelihood from raising crops on their own small parcels of land, as small merchants, or in tourist activities. There are some doctors and lawyers, but not many other professionals.

Since the War of 1967, most of the Palestinians have suffered economically due to unemployment, a tremendous rise in the cost of living, and taxation. Job opportunities are few because there are no industrial complexes in the Arab sectors. Moreover, many jobs are closed to Arabs for security reasons. When jobs can be found, they are as common day laborers with little or no opportunity to better either oneself or one's income. The well-organized tourist industry in Israel, aided by government subsidies, is under government control. Thus, in the majority of instances, the entire support for local Arabs is from the land. Even here, there is severe competition with organized and subsidized cooperatives and regulated prices. As for professional men, they find themselves cut off from either the means or the opportunities of practicing their profession as befits their training. The net result of all this is emigration or the desire to emigrate. To remedy the situation, there is a need for self-help programs, housing, funds for small, short-term loans to merchants and craftsmen, and more Christian tourists. The Grand Magisterium of the Order is addressing itself to these needs, heeding the voice of the Supreme Pontiff expressing his concern about the Christian presence and its future in the cradle of Christianity.

The Order is dedicated to fulfilling its purpose by directing its concern, interest, and efforts to a realistic approach to the economic and spiritual needs of the Christian community in the Holy Land by assisting the Latin Patriarchate. The Latin Patriarchate, having assumed responsibility for many activities that yield absolutely no profit, has been overburdened. This has resulted in a huge deficit that the Order has covered for many years. The majority of the suffering faithful are refugees or persons stricken by the catastrophe while many are migrants who have flocked from the villages to new centers of activity, where they often live in miserable conditions. Families are generally large but are too poor to be able to support their priests. From the very modest sum they receive from the Patriarchate to cover their meager personal expenses, the priests often share what they have with those in extreme distress.

The Patriarchate has a small annual contribution from the Custos, which must be used for certain purposes. It is extremely insufficient as it has not been increased to correspond with the increase in the needs of the Patriarchate. As an example, the budget for the schools is tragically insufficient to meet actual needs. The small grant by the Sacred Congregation for Oriental Churches has been barely changed since 1948, and its effective value has fallen due to changes in the rate of exchange.

The Patriarchate has no internal revenue to meet the demands for new equipment, construction, and repairs of churches, schools, workshops, and residences for sisters and priests, except for a small amount received in rentals for shops that it has built in the last few years.. In the last several years, the Equestrian Order of the Holy Sepulchre of Jerusalem has funded these projects through the voluntary contributions of the Lieutenancies of the Order in various countries. Through the generous contributions of the Lieutenancies, some major construction projects have been made. The Patriarchate rightfully expects the Order to meet the needs of its extraordinary budget for that is why the Order was constituted. The Grand Magisterium of the Order through its patrimony contributes a substantial sum annually that, with contributions from the Lieutenancies, funds the annual deficit. Even with this generous aid, there have been some vital projects delayed by lack of funds. With the continuous expansion of the Order, hope, too, grows that this condition can be alleviated.

There should be no difficulty in understanding that the maintenance and strengthening of the Catholic position in the Holy Land depends upon the aid offered by Catholics abroad. This has been true since the very beginning of the Church in Jerusalem. It is an Apostolic tradition as St. Paul informs us that the Christians from the nations of the world should come to the aid of the community in Jerusalem. It appears that it has been the will of Providence in every age that all Christians send alms to the Holy Land, and the Popes have constantly recommended these needs to the charity of the faithful.

# CHAPTER 8

# THE FRANCISCAN CUSTOS

Hard on the heels of the conquering crescent of Islam came the Cross of the Friars of St. Francis. The Cross on the glittering armor of the Crusaders had been short-lived in the Holy Land, but the brown-frocked Friars following in their wake stayed. Chauteaubriand, the celebrated French author, said of them:

> Alone—without defense among the ruins of Jerusalem, the Friars found in their Faith vigor to surmount many horrors and miseries. Nothing was strong enough to force them to abandon the tomb of Christ, neither depredation, ill treatment, menace nor death.

Although the Franciscans had been in Jerusalem since early 1219, their officially recognized presence dated from the bull addressed by Pope Gregory IX to the clergy of Palestine in 1230 charging them "to welcome the Friars and allow them to preach to the faithful and Holy Oratories and seminaries of their own." In 1333 there was officially established in Jerusalem the Franciscan Custody of Mt. Sion whose superior, The Guardian, became the Sovereign Pontiff's representative in the Holy Land. This was made possible by the King of Naples who paid the Sultan, 32,000 golden ducats in return for permission to establish the Brothers of the Franciscan Order in the Holy Land, who from that day have never left and where they still guard and care for the Holy Places.

In 1342, Pope Clement VI officially committed the care of the Holy Land to the Franciscans in the Bull "Gratias Agimus." In this way, the Order of the Holy Sepulchre (into which pilgrims were admitted) passed for six centuries into the hands of the Franciscans. The Franciscan superior in the Holy Land became the "Custos of the Holy Land."

In 1496, Pope Alexander VI, while reserving to himself and his successor the title of Supreme Head of the Order of the Holy Sepulchre, empowered the Franciscan Custodian of Mount Sion, the Commissary Apostolic of the Holy Land, with the privilege of conferring knighthood in the Order in the name of the Pope, just as long as the Latin Patriarchate remains vacant.

In the early days of the Guardian of the Franciscan Custos, accounts were written of the ceremony of investiture. It was necessary that investitures should take place in secret at night in the Basilica of the Holy Sepulchre. The Guardian vested in the Pontifical robes took his place at the altar and the candidate between two Franciscans, one holding the unsheathed sword and the other the golden spurs. The

*"St. Francis of Assisi Endeavors to Convert the Sultan"*
Gustav Doré (1832–1883) from *The History of the Crusades*
by Joseph François Michaud (1767–1839)

Guardian requested the candidate to kneel, put to him certain questions, handed him the spurs and dubbed him three times on the shoulder. That ceremony was preceded by the *Veni Creator* and concluded by softly singing the *Te Deum*. By the investiture of Knights and the keeping of a visible role, part of which has survived, the Franciscan Fathers helped greatly in assuring that the Order of the Holy Sepulchre continued to exist and prosper. Many pilgrims were received into the Order by the Custos. Since these Knights were not required to take the vows of celibacy, poverty, and obedience, and, since they did not live in a community, the Order was thus being transformed into a lay confraternity.

The Knights invested by the Guardian formed a military body who accepted certain rules of devotion. After returning to their own country they became closely associated with the priories there. The Knights did not forget the Custody and the Christians in the Holy Land to whom they constantly gave financial assistance. From this history, the Knights have retained a special regard and warmth for the Franciscans and the Custos.

It is interesting to note that certain ships were given the right by the Custodian of the Holy Land to fly the Jerusalem flag with the emblem of the five Crosses, which was also that of the Order of the Holy Sepulchre. This enabled pilgrims to travel in comparative safety to the Holy Land under the flag's protection.

The Christian world can never forget that the only Christian group existing in the very heart of Islam was the Franciscans who, weak and unarmed, were as hostages in the hands of the infidel. Frequently they had to endure cruel suffering in consequence. The history of the Custody is one of great courage, faith, and tenacity that can only be accounted for by their possessing immense resources of spiritual fortitude.

The Custody of the Holy Land assures the responsibilities of keeping watch over the sanctuaries in the Holy Places, equipping its own parishes, and caring for parish institutions. To these ends it receives the offerings of the faithful collected throughout the world on Good Friday. These offerings are inadequate. The Custody has therefore established an excellent system of Commissariats of the Holy Land. Scattered in the Christian world, they zealously sustain the work of the Custody in the Holy Places, their sanctuaries, parishes, schools, and welfare institutions.

*His Paternity Very Rev. Guiseppe Nazzaro, OFM, present Custos of the Holy Land*

# CHAPTER 9

# THE HOLY SEE AND
# THE HOLY LAND

His Holiness John Paul II made it clear that the Holy See supports the right of the Jewish people to a homeland, but it supports the same rights on the part of the Palestinian Arab people. The Vatican-Israel Fundamental Agreement states the principles of recognized religious freedom in Article 1:

1. The state of Israel, recalling its Declaration of Independence, affirms its continuing commitment to uphold and observe the human right to freedom of religion and conscience, as set forth in the Universal Declaration of Rights and in other international instruments to which it is a party.

2. The Holy See, recalling the Declaration on Religious Freedom of the Second Vatican Council, *Dignitatis Humanae*, affirms the Catholic Church's commitment to uphold the human right to freedom of religion and conscience, as set forth in the Universal Declaration of Human Rights and in other international instruments to which it is a party. The Holy See wishes to affirm as well the Catholic Church's respect for other religions and their followers as solemnly stated by the Second Vatican Council in its Declaration on the Relation of the Church to Non-Christian Religions, *Nostra Aetate.*

Pope John Paul II has commented on the problems associated with the Church's relationship with the Israeli government: "My thoughts are clear even without making them explicit. They are also thoughts which are linked to the tradition of the Holy See." His Holiness commented that one dimension of the problem is Jerusalem. "The Holy See has always held that it is a Holy Capital, a Holy City." Jerusalem is associated with three monotheistic religions: Judaism, Islam, and Christianity. "The second dimension regards... human rights of peoples. All peoples must have equal rights. I have a deep sense of the reality of the Holocaust, *Shoah.* I come from a country in which those things occurred with such brutality during the Second World War. It was genocide, people being slaughtered simply because they were Jews, because they belonged to that people. And so we feel that people have a right, but there are also the rights of other people, because other people exist, such as the Palestinian people."

His Holiness states in his Apostolic Letter, *Redemptionis Anno*:

> Jerusalem contains communities of believers full of life, whose presence the peoples of the whole world regard as a sign and source of hope—especially those who consider the Holy City to be in a certain way their spiritual heritage and a symbol of peace and harmony.
>
> Indeed, insofar as she is the homeland of the hearts of all the spiritual descendants of Abraham who hold her very dear, and the place where, according to faith, the created things of earth encounter the infinite transcendence of God, Jerusalem stands out as a symbol of coming together, of union and of universal peace for the human family.

His Holiness commented that Christians honor Jerusalem with a religious and intense concern because there the great events of the Redemption were accomplished—the Passion, Death and Resurrection of our Lord Jesus Christ. The first Christian community sprang up in Jerusalem and remained throughout the centuries "a continual ecclesial presence despite difficulties."

His Holiness emphasized that Jews love Jerusalem and in every age venerate her memory because there remained many monuments from the time of David and of Solomon who built the temple. He remarked that Muslims call Jerusalem "Holy" with a profound attachment that goes back to the origin of Islam and springs from the many special places of pilgrimage. Moreover, for over a thousand years they dwelt there without interruption.

The Holy Father maintains that Jerusalem should be a unique international city with international guarantees as evident in his remark: "There should be found, with good will and farsightedness, a concrete and just solution by which different interests and aspirations can be provided for in a harmonious and stable form, and be safeguarded in an adequate and efficacious manner by a special statute internationally guaranteed so that no party could jeopardize it."

His Holiness asks for the desired security for the Jewish people in the Holy Land who wish to preserve testimonies to their history and their faith. He also says that the Palestinians in the Holy Land, who have historical roots there and for decades have been dispersed, have the natural right in justice to have a homeland and to be able to live in peace and tranquility with the other people of the area.

The Vatican Secretary of State issued statements in May 1996 to clarify the Holy See's position on the Palestinian situation in Jerusalem. This position underwrites the Vatican-Israel Fundamental Agreement and is firm in the recognition of the political reality that is present:

> There exists a territorial problem relative to Jerusalem. Since 1967, when a part of the City was militarily occupied and then annexed, this problem has become more obvious and more difficult. The part of the city that was occupied and annexed is where most of the Holy Places of the three monotheistic religions are situated.
>
> The Holy See has always insisted that this territorial question should be resolved equitably and by negotiation. The Holy See, as the previ-

*His Holiness Pope John Paul II*

ously mentioned Article 1 of the Fundamental Agreement indicates, is not concerned with the question of how many square meters or kilometers constitute the disputed territory, but it does have the right—a right that it exercises—to express a moral judgement on the situation.

It is obvious that every territorial dispute involves ethical considerations, such as the right of national communities to self-determination, the right of communities to preserve their own identity, the right of all people to equality before the law and in the distribution of resources, the right not to be discriminated against by reason of ethnic origin or religious affiliation, etc.

The Holy See's attitude with regard to the territorial situation of Jerusalem is necessarily the same as that of the international community. The latter could be summarized as follows: the part of the City militarily occupied in 1967 and subsequently annexed and declared the Capital of the State of Israel, is occupied territory, and all Israeli measures that exceed the power of a belligerent occupant under international law are therefore null and void. In particular, this same position was expressed, and is still expressed, by Resolution 478 of the United Nations Security Council, adopted on 20 August 1980, which declared the Israeli "basic law" concerning Jerusalem to be "null and void," and which invited countries with Embassies in Jerusalem to move them elsewhere.

As is well known, when the Holy See entered into diplomatic relations with the State of Israel, it opened its Nunciature (Embassy) in Old Jaffa, where indeed the overwhelming majority of the Embassies are situated. It is also well known that the Apostolic Delegation for Jerusalem and Palestine (opened on 11 February 1948, before the State of Israel was established) continues to function under the present Apostolic Pro-Nuncio, who is also the Apostolic Delegate to Jerusalem and Palestine.

There is however a further aspect of Jerusalem that in the Holy See's view goes well beyond the simple territorial aspect: this is the "religious dimension" of the City, the particular value that it has for the Jewish, Christian, and Muslim believers who live there, and for Jewish, Christian, and Muslim believers throughout the world.

It is a question here of a value that must be considered as having a worldwide and universal character: Jerusalem is a "treasure of humanity."

For decades (long before the 1967 occupation), the Holy See has always been very attentive to this aspect and has not failed to intervene when necessary, insisting on the need for adequate measures to protect the singular identity of the Holy City. An explanation of what this protection consists of, and what characteristics it must have in order to meet its objectives, can be outlined as follows:

a) With a view to safeguarding the universal character of a City already claimed by two peoples (Arab and Jewish) and held sacred by three religions, the Holy See supported the proposal for the internationalization of the territory, the "corpus separatum" called for by U.N. General Assembly Resolution 181 (II) of 29 November 1947. The Holy See at the time considered the "corpus separatum" as an adequate means, a useful juridical instrument, for preventing Jerusalem from becoming a cause and arena of conflict, with the resulting loss of an important aspect of its identity (as in fact subsequently happened and continues to happen).

b) In the years that followed, although the objective of internationalization was shown to be unattainable, the Holy See—especially, but not only, through public statements of the Popes—continued to call for the protection of the Holy City's identity. It consistently drew attention to the need for an international commitment in this regard. To this end, the Holy See has consistently called for an international juridical instrument, which is what is meant by the phrase "an internationally guaranteed special statute."

# CHAPTER 10

# NATIVE CHRISTIANS OF THE HOLY LAND

Knights and Ladies of the Equestrian Order of the Holy Sepulchre of Jerusalem recognize their responsibility to the future of the Holy Land. Even though the Holy Land is only a small part of the vast region of the Middle East, it has great religious significance. From the history of the past forty years, we know that war or peace in the Middle East, and possibly in all of the world, depends largely upon the future of the Holy Land. The future that should be secured in distributive justice for all including the native Christians may be lost if injustice is generated in the struggle between Judaism and Islam.

Consider the lessons learned when an advanced Western civilization lands on the shores of another geographic region. Its members seize territory and displace the native peoples. Direct wars are eventually waged within a pattern of cultural conflict. The native peoples are marginalized and suffer from the poverty eventuating from injustice. This was America in the first centuries of its founding. This is Israel in the first decades of its founding. Americans understand this pattern and the horrid consequences that our actions have had on Native Americans. Americans are striving to undo the damage we inflicted. This also gives American Knights and Ladies of the Holy Sepulchre of Jerusalem a clear perspective when reviewing the plight of the native Christians of the Holy Land.

Facts strongly indicate that Christians and Muslims living in Israel and the Occupied Territories are being systematically deprived of their homelands. A report by a Special Committee of the United Nations was prepared to investigate Israeli practices affecting the human rights of the population in the Occupied Territory. This report covered the years ending in August 31, 1981 but received little publicity. It detailed a series of human rights violations inflicted upon the Christian and Muslim population by the Israeli occupying forces. These violations continue to this day. Israeli take land from Christians and Muslims declaring certain land as "state land" and closed for security reasons. Many parcels of land are confiscated outright and many homes demolished. The record shows that since 1967, more than 1,300 houses have been demolished by the Israeli government.

The Church has constantly been concerned about the situation in the Holy Land, particularly in Jerusalem. Pope Paul VI pointedly noted the relationship of Christians in the Holy Land. His Holiness said, "were their presence to cease, the shrines would be without the warmth of this living witness, and the Christian Holy Places of Jerusalem and the Holy Land would become like museums. We have already had occasion to express openly our anxiety at the decreasing numbers of Christians in the ancient regions that were the cradle of our Faith." Pope John Paul II expressed the same sentiments.

The primary question is what is to become of the people, the native Christians of the Holy Land. It has been said, and rightly so, that peace depends upon the historical balance of the three peoples—Jews, Christians, and Muslims—living in their common historic homeland. The preservation of Christianity in the Holy Land to which the Order pledges assistance depends upon the Christians who remain within the Holy Land. Without them, there can be no peace and without them the Holy Places would become impersonal monuments. Such is the challenge to the Order, not only because of the unjust treatment of the native Christians, but because they seek greater freedom to find adequate housing for their families, employment to earn a basic living, and educational opportunities for their children. The Order is cognizant of the situation and is now addressing the problem of housing and employment . Education has had the principal attention of the Order and will continue to do so. This leaves the problem of greater freedom that must be addressed by individuals in their own countries in an endeavor to shield the native Christian population from this deprivation.

The Constitution of the Order gives the aims of the Order:

> *To strengthen in its members the practice of Christian Life, in absolute fidelity to the Supreme Pontiff and according to the teaching of the Church, observing as its foundation the principles of charity of which the Order is a fundamental means for assistance to the Holy Land;*

> *To sustain and aid the charitable, cultural and social works and institutions of the Catholic Church in the Holy Land, particularly those of and in the Latin Patriarchate of Jerusalem, with which the Order maintains traditional ties;*

> *To support the preservation and propagation of the Faith in those lands, being interested in this work Catholics scattered throughout the world are united in charity by the symbol of the Order with all our Brother and Sister Christians;*

> *To sustain the rights of the Catholic Church in the Holy Land.*

We have witnessed the founding of a Jewish state in the Holy Land. We are witnessing a replacement of a native society rather than a just integration of a native population. Through this ordeal, native Christians are being shielded by the work of the Patriarch facilitated by the aid of the Order of the Holy Sepulchre. However, we have had only a limited success, but with God's grace, justice shall prevail.

History records a dramatic change in the population. In 1922, the population of

Palestine was: Christians—73,000; Jews—84,000; Muslims—591,000. There was a significant change in the population due to the natural birth rate and the immigration of Jews under the British administration. In 1947, the population of Israel and Palestine was: Christians—146,000; Jews—614,000; Muslims—1,091,000. In 1990, the population of Israel and Palestine was: Christians—155,000; Jews—3,729,000; Muslims—1,999,000.

Figures for the native Christians show the deleterious effects of cultural conflict resulting in emigration. Those for the Jews show the massive immigration, primarily from Eastern Europe. Those for the Muslims show the forcible displacement as refugees from their homelands.

All Christians and particularly Knights and Ladies of the Order of the Holy Sepulchre are called upon to provide economic assistance, time, and talent to support programs in process and to develop new programs that will maintain the Christian presence in the Holy Land. It is hoped that as the Order reaches and passes the 900th anniversary of its founding, it will be able to announce that it is meeting successfully the challenges that confront it today.

# II

## Administration
## and Privileges
## of the Order

*But this the scope was of our former thought,*
*Of Sion's fort to scale the noble wall,*
*The Christian folk from bondage to have brought,*
*Wherein, alas, they long have lived thrall,*
*In Palestine an empire to have wrought,*
*Where godliness might reign perpetual,*
*And none be left, that pilgrim might denay*
*To see Christ's tomb, and promised vows to pay.*

*Jerusalem Delivered* by Torquato Tasso (1544–1595)
translated by Edward Fairfax (1560–1635)
First Book, Stanza XXIII

## CHAPTER 11

# ORGANIZATION OF THE ORDER

The Equestrian Order of the Holy Sepulchre of Jerusalem is an integrated person within the Catholic Church's structure, and is listed in the *Annuario Pontificio* issued annually by the Vatican. It is under the protection of the Holy See. Specifically it is under the personal protection of the reigning Pontiff. The Pope appoints a Cardinal to be Grand Master. All appointments in the Order are made by this office in virtue of the power conferred upon it by the Pope. Recent Pontiffs have held the Order in such high esteem that the Grand Master has been among the most respected members of the Curia. The headquarters of the Order is located within the boundaries of the Vatican in the Palazzo Della Rovere.

Revised statutes (Constitution) approved by Pope Paul VI on July 19, 1977, and affirmed by Pope John Paul II, prescribe the organization of the Order as well as the grades of Knighthood, their qualifications, prerogatives, and duties. The Order operates through Lieutenancies as may from time to time be constituted, each with territorial jurisdiction. In March 1996, a Lieutenancy was established in Poland.

The Order is directed and governed by the Cardinal Grand Master, assisted by the Grand Magisterium and its presidency along with the Council. The Grand Magisterium is composed of the Cardinal Grand Master, the Lieutenant General, the Governor General, the Vice Governor Generals, the Chancellor, and Master of Ceremonies. There are no more than twelve in number of which at least two-thirds are laymen. All have the title of Excellency.

The Governor General, the Vice Governor Generals, the Chancellor, and members of the Grand Magisterium designated by the Cardinal Grand Master constitute the Presidency. In practice the Presidency is not convened. The Latin Patriarch of Jerusalem is the Grand Prior of the Order, because of the historic and spiritual connection of the Order to the Holy Land. The spiritual seat of the Order is Jerusalem. Its mother church is St. Onofrio in Rome.

A prelate approved by the Cardinal Grand Master and approved by the Supreme Pontiff serves as "Assessor."

The Council is called and provided for by the Cardinal Grand Master, who determines the agenda. In practice the meeting of the Council, called the Consulta, is called every four years. Taking part in the Consulta is the Patriarch Grand Prior, Assessor, members of the Grand Magisterium, Lieutenants, a representative of the Secretary of State to His Holiness, and a representative designated by the Sacred Congregation for the Eastern Churches. A newly formed Lieutenancy in its forma-

Dignitaries at the 1982 Consulta. From left to right: H.E. Angelo Di Giorgio, KGCHS, member of the Grand Magisterium (now deceased); H.E. Alfred J. Blasco, KGCHS, Vice Governor General (now Honorary Vice Governor General and Knight of the Collar); H.E. Prince Paolo Enrico Massimo Lancellotti, KGCHS, Governor General (now Lieutenant General and Knight of the Collar); His Eminence Maximilian Cardinal de Furstenberg, Grand Master (now deceased); His Holiness Pope John Paul II; H.E. Most Rev. Msgr. André Jacques Fougerat, KGCHS, Assessor (now deceased); H.E. Count Peter Wolff-Metternich Zur Gracht, KGCHS, Vice Governor General (now Knight of the Collar); H.E. Msgr. Mario Carlomagno, KCHS, Chancellor (now deceased); Dr. Walter Fanfani, KC*HS, member of the Grand Magisterium (now retired).

tive stage is called a Magistral Delegation headed by a Magistral Delegate who also attends the Consulta.

A commission composed of three members of the Grand Magisterium is named by the Cardinal Grand Master to examine nominations and promotions in the Order. Other temporary and consulting Commissions may be appointed to study, plan, and program works and activities in the Holy Land.

The life of the Order is articulated in the individual nations through local divisions, called Lieutenancies or Magistral Delegations, which may have Sections, local Delegations, or Regional Representatives.

For its organization and fulfillment of its works, the Order receives bequests, offerings, and contributions from the Lieutenancies and Magistral Delegations. All such amounts go directly to the Holy Land by way of the Grand Magisterium in Rome. The Grand Magisterium in Rome manages its own patrimony, the income of which is more than sufficient to cover its operating expenses plus a substantial gift to the Holy Land yearly. All dignitaries of the Order in the Grand Magisterium and the Lieutenancies serve without compensation. The financial reports of the Grand Magisterium are reviewed by a College of Auditors composed of three members appointed by the Cardinal Grand Master.

The listing of the Grand Magisterium in 1998 follows:

His Eminence, Carlo Cardinal Furno
 Cardinal Grand Master
 Knight of the Collar

His Beatitude, Michel Sabbah, Latin Patriarch of Jerusalem
 Grand Prior
 Knight of the Collar

His Excellency, Most Reverend Luigi del Gallo Roccagiovine
 Assessor
 Knight Commander With Star

His Excellency, Prince Paola Enrico Massimo Lancellotti
 Lieutenant General
 Knight of the Collar

His Excellency, Count Ludovico Carducci Artenisio,
 Governor General
 Knight of the Collar

His Excellency, Count Peter Wolff-Metternich zur Gracht
 Vice Governor General
 Knight of the Collar

His Excellency, F. Russell Kendall
 Vice Governor General
 Knight of the Collar

His Excellency, Sir Alfred J. Blasco
  Vice Governor General Emeritus
  Knight of the Collar

Gr. Uff. General Ferruccio Ferrari
  Chancellor
  Knight Grand Cross

Reverend Monsignor Bernard de Lanversin
  Master of Ceremonies
  Knight Commander with Star

Other Members of the Grand Magisterium: H.E. Gr. Uff. Count Prof. Guiseppe Dalla Torre Del Tempio Di Sanguinetto, KGCHS; H.E. Most Rev. Thomas G. Doran, KC*HS; H.E. M. Philippe Husson, KCHS; H.E. Theo W. van Nierop, KGCHS; H.E. Prof. Dr. Franz Eckert, KGCHS; H.E. Frau Elizabeth Verreet, LGCHS; H.E. Count Prof. Aldo Maria Arena, KGCHS; H.E. Gr. Uff. Count Prof. Agostino Borromeo, KGCHS; H.E. Robert H. Benson, KGCHS; H.E. Mary Anne Sansone, LC*HS.

The Constitution of the Order requires of its members:

- Religious devotion
- Participation in the activities of the Church
- Lay Apostolate placing themselves at the service of the Church
- Diligence of the ecumenical spirit by means of active interest in the well recognized problems of the Holy Land

The Order today is divided into four classes: Knight and Lady of the Grand Cross; Knight and Lady Commander with Star; Knight and Lady Commander; Knight and Lady.

Knights and Ladies are chosen from "among persons of Catholic faith and of flawless moral conduct, who are particularly praiseworthy on behalf of the Catholic works of the Holy Land." The rank of Knight or Lady of the Collar, rarely given, is conferred on "the most eminent persons, ecclesiastic or lay, of the highest dignity, in the most exceptional cases."

For persons of unquestionable moral conduct and particularly meritorious charity on behalf of the Holy Land, even if they cannot assume the duties that the investiture imposes on Knights and Ladies, insignia of Merit with the following classes may be awarded:Cross of Merit of the Holy Sepulchre of Jerusalem; Cross of Merit with Silver or Gold Star of the Holy Sepulchre of Jerusalem.

Two special distinctions of the Order are 1) Palm of Jerusalem of Gold, Silver, or Bronze can be conferred by the Cardinal Grand Master to persons of flawless moral conduct, especially meritorious on behalf of the Order or of the Holy Land. This honor can also be conferred for the same reasons by the Patriarch Grand Prior to persons with established residence in the Holy Land and in exceptional cases to persons in transit there. 2) Pilgrim Shell granted by the Cardinal Grand Master or by the Latin Patriarch Grand Prior to members who have completed a pious Pilgrimage to the Holy Land.

The religious character of the Order of the Holy Sepulchre of Jerusalem is obvious not only in its objectives and requirements for admission, but also in the ceremonial investiture of its newly elected Knights. This ecclesiastical ceremony combines a profession of faith with the ancient ritual used for the conferral of knighthood. The candidates do not take monastic vows, but promise to live an upright Christian life in accordance with the Commandments of God and the precepts of the Roman Catholic Church: in absolute spiritual fealty to the Supreme Pontiff, as true soldiers of Christ.

# CHAPTER 12

# LIEUTENANCIES OF THE ORDER

Lieutenancies of the Equestrian Order of the Holy Sepulchre of Jerusalem and their Lieutenants and Grand Priors exist in the following countries (48 in 29 countries):

**Argentina**

H.E. Prof. Dr. Isidoro J. Ruiz Moreno, KCHS
H.E. Most Rev. Hector R. Aguer, KC*HS

**Australia**

Western

H.E. Clifford Holloway, KGCHS
H.E. Most Rev. Barry J. Hickey, KC*HS

Eastern

H.E. Costandi Bastoli, KCHS
H.E. Edward Cardinal Clancy, KGCHS

Southern

H.E. Donald Trescowthick, KCHS
H.E. Most Rev. Peter J. Connors, KC*HS

**Austria**

H.E. Dr. Otto Kaspar, KGCHS
H.E. Abt Maximilian Fürnsinn, KCHS

**Belgium**

H.E. Count Claude Carpenter de Changy, KGCHS
H.E. Most Rev. Paul Lanneau, KC*HS

**Brazil**

Rio De Janeiro

H.E. Gilson Araujo, KC*HS
H.E. Most Rev. Francisco José Maria Vasconcellos, KC*HS

San Paolo

H.E. Joao Baptista Isnard, KCHS
H.E. Most Rev. Hugo Munari, KC*HS

## Canada

Montreal
H.E. Jean-Pierre LaFerriere, KGCHS
H.E. Most Rev. Andre Marie Cimchella, OSM, KC*HS
Quebec
H.E. Jacques Coté, KGCHS
H.E. Most Rev. Maurice Couture, KC*HS
Toronto
H.E. Dr. R. Gerald Guest, KC*HS
H.E. Most Rev. Aloysius M. Ambrozic, KC*HS
Vancouver
H.E. William E. Whelan, KCHS
H.E. Most Rev. Adam Exner, KC*HS

## Colombia

H.E. Ricardo Triana Uribe, KGCHS
H.E. Most Rev. Arturo Franco Arango, KC*HS

## Ecuador

H.E. Vincente Norero y de Luca, KGCHS
H.E. Most Rev. Bernardino Echeverria Ruiz, KC*HS

## England and Wales

H.E. David Hirst, KGCHS
H.E. Most Rev. Michael Bowen, KC*HS

## Finland

H.E. Alhard Eckstein, KCHS
H.E. Most Rev. Paul Verschuren, KCHS

## France

H.E. General Count Louis d'Harcourt, KGCHS
H.E. Most Rev. Jacques Perrier, KC*HS

## Germany

H.E. Dr. Peter Heidinger, KGCHS
H.E. Most Rev. Anton Schlenbach, KC*HS

## Gilbraltar

Magistral Delegate Augustus Stagnetto, KGCHS
H.E. Most Rev. Bernard Devlin, KC*HS

## Holland

H.E. Jan H.J. Daniels, KC*HS
H.E. Most Rev. Josephus Franciscus Lescrauwaet, KC*HS

**Hungary**
Magistral Delegate Prof. Geza Erszegi, KHS
H.E. Laszlo Cardinal Paskai, KC*HS

**Ireland**
H.E. Michael D.Mc Grath, KGCHS
H.E. Most Rev. Sean Brady, KCHS

**Italy**
Central
H.E. Count Mario Cantuti Castelvetri, KGCHS
H.E. Most Rev. Giovanni De Andrea, KC*HS, Apostolic Nuncio
Southern
H.E. Francesco Zippitelli, KGCHS
H.E. Most Rev. Mariano Magrassi, KC*HS
Northern
H.E. Pier Luigi Parola, KGCHS
H.E. Most Rev. Libero Tresoldi, KC*HS
Sicily
H.E. Prof. Antonio Mistretta, KGCHS
H.E. Salvatore Cardinal Pappalardo, KC*HS

**Luxembourg**
Lieutenant to be appointed
H.E. Most Rev. Fernand Franck, KC*HS

**Malta**
Magistral Delegate H.E. Louis Gera Lauron Testaferrata
H.E. Most Rev. Emanuele Gerada

**Mexico**
H.E. Fernando Uribe Calderon, KC*HS
H.E. Ernesto Cardinal Corripio Ahumada, KGCHS

**Monaco**
H.E. Cesar Charles Solamito, KGCHS
H.E. Most Rev. Joseph Sardou, KC*HS

**Phillipines**
H.E. Carlos Ledesma, KGCHS
H.E. Jaime Cardinal Sin, KGCHS

**Poland**
H.E. Jerzy Wojtczak, KHS
H.E. Josef Cardinal Glemp, KGCHS

**Portugal**
  H.E. Edwardo Norte Santos Silva, KGCHS
  H.E. Antonio Cardinal Ribeiro, KGCHS

**Puerto Rico**
  H.E. Luis F. Sala, KGCHS
  H.E. Most Rev. Juan Fremiot Torres Oliver, KC*HS

**Scotland**
  H.E. Capt. David Ogilvy Fairlie of Myres, KCHS
  H.E. Thomas Joseph Cardinal Winning, KGCHS

**Spain**
  Barcelona
      H.E. José Maria de Quadrasy de Caralt, KGCHS
      H.E. Most Rev. Elias Yanes Alvarez
  Madrid [Castille y Leon]
      H.E. Don Gonzalo de Mora y Aragon, KGCHS
      H.E. Most Rev. José M. Estepa Llaurens, KC*HS

**Switzerland**
  H.E. Werner O. Ciocarelli, KGCHS
  H.E. Henri Cardinal Schwery, KGCHS

**Taiwan**
  Magistral Delegate to be chosen
  H.E. Most Rev. Joseph Ti-Kang, KCHS

**United States**
  Southeastern
      H.E. George H. Toye, KGCHS
      H.E. Most Rev. Francis B. Schulte, KC*HS
  Middle Atlantic
      H.E. Bernard J. Ficarra, KGCHS
      H.E. James Cardinal Hickey, KGCHS
  Eastern
      H.E. Martin J. Moran, KGCHS
      H.E. John Cardinal O'Connor, KGCHS
  Northeastern
      H.E. George T. Ryan, KGCHS
      H.E. Bernard Cardinal Law, KGCHS
  North Central
      H.E. Matthew J. Lamb, KGCHS
      H.E. Francis Cardinal George, OMI, KC*HS

Northern
    H.E. William B. Guyol, KGCHS
    H.E. Most Rev. Justin F. Rigali, KC*HS
Southwestern
    H.E. Albin J. Brezna, KGCHS
    H.E. Most Rev. Rene Gracida, KC*HS
Western
    H.E. George G. Zorn, KGCHS
    H.E. Roger Cardinal Mahony, KGCHS
Northwestern
    H.E. Albert Maggio, KGCHS
    H.E. Most Rev. John R. Quinn, KCHS

Total Confreres and Consoeurs of the Equestrian Order of the Holy Sepulchre of Jerusalem at the end of 1997 was approximately 19,000, of which almost half were from the United States. This represents a growth of 36% world-wide in the past six years.

*Coat of Arms of the Order*

# CHAPTER 13

# GRAND MASTERS
# OF THE ORDER

In the early centuries, crowned heads of Europe were the Grand Masters of the Order of the Holy Sepulchre of Jerusalem. The government of the Order over the current century was entrusted to a Cardinal although there were times when the Latin Patriarch of Jerusalem acted in that capacity. During the reign of Pope Saint Pius X, 1903 to 1914, Pope Saint Pius X himself took over as Grand Master. Today the Order is directed and governed by a Cardinal Grand Master appointed by the Supreme Pontiff. He is assisted principally by the Governor General and the Grand Magisterium. He, as the Constitution of the Order states, represents the Order, insures application and observance of the Constitution, and arranges what he considers necessary or useful for attainment of the goals of the Order, by means of binding directives.

The Cardinal Grand Master is responsible for direct relations of the Order with the Supreme Pontiff and highest Church and civil authorities, international and national. He can delegate dignitaries of the Grand Magisterium, or Lieutenants and Magistral Delegates in the territory of their jurisdiction, to perform specific duties.

For 600 years, there were thirty-five crowned heads in hereditary succession as Grand Masters of the Military Order of the Holy Sepulchre, now known as the Equestrian Order of the Holy Sepulchre of Jerusalem. These spanned the years from Godfrey de Bouillon in 1099 to Charles II, King of Spain, Naples, and Sicily in 1700.

| | |
|---|---|
| 1099 | Godfrey de Bouillon, Duke of Lower Lorraine, Overlord of the Crusader States, Advocate of the Holy Sepulchre |
| 1100 | Baldwin I, the brave, brother of Godfrey de Bouillon, Second Overlord of the Crusader States, First King of Jerusalem |
| 1118 | Baldwin II, the irreproachable, Third Overlord of the Crusader States, Second King of Jerusalem at the zenith of the Crusader States |
| 1134 | Fulck of Anjou, the Red, Fourth Overlord of the Crusader States, Third King of Jerusalem |
| 1143 | Baldwin III, the strong, Fourth King of Jerusalem |
| 1162 | Amalric I, brother of Baldwin III, Fifth King of Jerusalem |

| | |
|---|---|
| 1173 | Baldwin IV, the leper, Sixth King of Jerusalem |
| 1183 | Baldwin V, the boy, Seventh King of Jerusalem |
| 1184 | Sibylla, mother of Baldwin V, Queen of Jerusalem |
| 1186 | Guy of Lusignan, husband of Sibylla, Last King of Jerusalem |
| 1188 | Henry, Count of Champagne |
| 1195 | John, Earl of Brienne |
| 1208 | Frederick II, German Emperor |
| 1250 | Conrad, elder son of Frederick II |
| 1252 | Manfred, son of Frederick II |
| 1265 | Charles of Anjou, named by Pope Honorius III |
| 1285 | Charles II, son of Charles of Anjou |
| 1309 | Robert, third son of Charles of Anjou |
| 1342 | Louis, Prince of Taranto, brother of Robert |
| 1382 | Charles III, Duke of Durazzo |
| 1386 | Ladislaus |
| 1414 | Joanna II, ruled in the person of James of Norbonne, her husband |
| 1438 | various Grand Masters over four years between René of Anjou and Alphonse of Aragon |
| 1442 | Alphonse V, King of Aragon and Sicily |
| 1458 | Ferdinand, son of Alphonse V, after much controversy with members of the House of Anjou |
| 1493 | Alphonse II, Duke of Calabria, son of Ferdinand |
| 1494 | Ferdinand, son af Alphonse II |
| 1495 | Frederick, uncle of Ferdinand |
| 1501 | Ferdinand II |
| 1516 | Charles of Hapsburg |
| 1555 | Philip II, son of Charles of Hapsburg |
| 1598 | Philip III, King of Spain |
| 1621 | Philip IV, King of Spain |
| 1667 | Charles II, King of Spain |

In the ensuing years the Knights of the Holy Sepulchre lived close to their priories in their own country, looking for protection to their own King or Prince as Grand Master. The Guardian of the Franciscan Custody of the Holy Land represented the Supreme Pontiff. This is evidenced by the bull in 1708 authorizing the Guardian to invest new Knights. Again in 1746, the bull of Pope Benedict XIV reconfirmed the authorization for the Guardian of the Custody of the Holy Land to continue investing knights into the Order who were present in Jerusalem.

Actually, from 1496 until the restoration of the Latin Patriarchate in 1847, faithful custodians of the Holy Land conferred the honors of Knighthood on the deserving. Pope Pius IX in December 1847 transferred to the Latin Patriarch of Jerusalem the right to appoint Knights of the Holy Sepulchre, and to act as Grand Master.

At thirty-four years of age, Most Reverend Joseph Valerga was appointed the Latin Patriarch of Jerusalem in October 1847 by Pope Pius IX. His untimely death occurred on December 2, 1872 after only four days illness. Upon the death of Patriarch Valerga, Most Reverend Vincent Bracco was appointed Patriarch in 1873. He died on June 19, 1889 after sixteen years in office.

*Carlo Cardinal Furno, Grand Master*
(A. Mari, L'Osservator Romano)

Pope Leo XIII then appointed Most Reverend Louis Piavi as Patriarch to succeed Patriarch Bracco and to act as Grand Master. The highlight of the Patriarch's reign was the Eucharistic Congress of 1893 held in the co-Cathedral of the Most Holy Name of Jesus. This resulted in the solution of many problems prevailing in the Holy Land and the development of a bond of understanding and unity between the Latin and Oriental religious. On January 24, 1905, Patriarch Piavi died after fifteen years of wonderful service.

It was in 1906 that the Most Reverend Philip Camassei became the Latin Patriarch of Jerusalem. On May 3, 1907 Pope St. Pius X reserved to himself and successors the title of Grand Master and appointed the Latin Patriarch of Jerusalem as Administrator of the Order. Patriarch Camassei became a Cardinal in December 1919. Exhausted by ill treatment at the hands of the Muslims, he died on January 18, 1921

The disasters of World War I confronted Most Reverend Louis Barlassina when he succeeded Patriarch Camassei in 1920 as the Latin Patriarch of Jerusalem. However, upon the elevation of Patriarch Camassei to the Cardinalate, Barlassina served as Apostolic Administrator and Rector (Grand Master of the Order).

With the Balfour Declaration, a Jewish national homeland was mandated in Palestine. This resulted in conflicts with the result that Muslims and native

Christians were either displaced or marginalized. Revolts resulted in many deaths. Many looked to Patriarch Barlassina as peacemaker and mediator between the immigrant Jews and the native Christians. The increasing responsibilities of the vast Archdiocese hung heavy on the shoulders of Patriarch Barlassina: maintaining and improving the existing missions, building new missions, supporting the missionaries, and constructing and supporting hospitals, schools, and homes for the aged, the sick, and the poor. Nevertheless, the Order flourished under the rectorship of Patriarch Barlassina. In January, 1928, Pope Pius XI decreed that the Order remain under the protection of the Holy See, but the Patriarch was to be Rector and Apostolic Administrator of the Order with full governance over it.

On July 1940 Pope Pius XII decreed that a Cardinal Protector of the Order should be the Grand Master. He appointed His Eminence Nicholas Cardinal Canali as Grand Master. He was succeeded in 1962 by His Eminence Eugene Cardinal Tisserant who for many years was Dean of the College of Cardinals. Upon Cardinal Tisserant's death in 1972, Pope Paul VI appointed His Eminence Maximilian Cardinal De Furstenberg to be the third Cardinal Grand Master. At that point the Order was electrified by the superb and masterful administration of the Cardinal, ably assisted by Prince Paolo Enrico Lancellotti, Knight of the Collar, who was appointed Governor General in 1976.

Cardinal de Furstenberg in his fourteen years as Cardinal Grand Master, left a remarkable record of accomplishments for the Holy Land and the Order that is difficult to equal. Cardinal de Furstenberg's administration resulted in:

> Contributions from Lieutenancies of the Order increased 10.26 times with an average annual increase of 73%.

> Income from Patrimony of the Order increased 11.97 times with an average annual increase of 83%.

> Funds to the Holy Land for purposes of the Order increased 11.68 times with an average annual increase of 83%.

On December 4, 1988, His Eminence Joseph Cardinal Caprio was appointed Grand Master of the Order by Pope John Paul II. The Order was most fortunate to have Cardinal Caprio as its Grand Master who came into the office with many years of distinguished service to the Church. After his ordination as a priest on December 17, 1938, and his studies at the Pontifical Ecclesiastical Academy, he was called to the Secretariat of State, Vatican City. He saw service in China, Belgium, Vietnam, Taiwan, and India. In 1961 he was appointed Archbishop of Apollonia, and in the same year received his episcopal ordination. For eight years prior to 1977, he served as Secretary of the Administration of the Patrimony of the Holy See. For two years following, Pope Paul VI appointed him Undersecretary of State. He was created a Cardinal in June 1979 when he became President of the Patrimony of the Holy See. Two years thereafter, he became Prefect of the Economic Affairs of the Holy See, and served in that post until his appointment in 1988 as Grand Master of the Order.

Under the guidance of Cardinal Caprio, the number of Knights and Ladies through-out the world has multiplied. This has made possible a substantial increase in dona-tions for charitable works in the Holy Land.

Carlo Cardinal Furno was appointed Grand Master in 1996. He had a most appropriate background. In 1960, His Eminence was assigned as Secretary in the Apostolic Delegation of Jerusalem. Two years later he served with the Secretary of State, the Section of Extraordinary Ecclesiastical Affairs, responsible for Palestine and the Middle East. In the following eleven years he grew in wisdom and under-standing of the situation in the Holy Land. Moreover, he served as the Apostolic Nuncio of Lebanon from 1978 to 1982. Cardinal Furno brings to the Order a com-prehensive knowledge of the present problems in the Holy Land. His clear thinking on the economic needs of the Latin Patriarchate are superb. He has undertaken the vast burden of repairing the Palazzo Della Rovere, which is the headquarters of the Equestrian Order of the Holy Sepulchre of Jerusalem. This edifice is an architectural jewel completed for occupancy in 1492 for Giovanni Cardinal Della Rovere, broth-er to Pope Sixtus IV (Francesco Della Rovere who reigned from 1471 to 1484). The Palazzo is approximately 200 yards from St. Peter's Basilica.

# CHAPTER 14

# GOVERNOR GENERALS OF THE ORDER

An Apostolic Brief is an important document issued by the Pope. It begins with the name of the Pontiff and a greeting such as "To you beloved son, good health and my Apostolic Blessing," or with the words "in perpetual memory." It has a special seal, impressed on wax since decades past, and colored red. The seal is called "The Seal of the Fisherman," referring to the occupation of St. Peter and the Apostles. Circling this seal is the name of the reigning Pontiff.

Such a document was issued on December 8, 1962 by Pope John XXIII revising the Constitution of the Equestrian Order of the Holy Sepulchre of Jerusalem. According to Ameleto Cardinal Cicognani, Secretary of State, the Cardinal Grand Master of the Order had requested the revision to adapt the Constitution to modern times. In the Apostolic Brief, the Pope approved, confirmed and invested with the Apostolic Sanction, the new Constitution of the Equestrian Order of the Holy Sepulchre of Jerusalem. This historical document eloquently expressed the love of the Holy Father for the Order and the solicitous protection granted by the Holy See. It was a source of life and energy for members of the Order.

The revised Constitution provided for a Grand Magisterium composed of a Lieutenant General, a referendarius, and a Grand Master of Ceremonies, the first two chosen from lay members and the third from the ecclesiastic ranks. The Lieutenant General, chosen from the Lieutenants of the Order, was designated assistant to the Cardinal Grand Master, primarily to represent him in his absence or when he could not preside. The first Lieutenant General appointed was Prince Don Carlos Ludovico Gonzaga de Vescovado.

The referendarius was given the duties of supervision of the offices of the Grand Magisterium and ordinary activities of the Lieutenancies. This office was the fore-runner of the office of what is now the Governor General. Marquis Mario Mochi was appointed Referendius Perpetuus. Mochi had been a member of the Milan Lieutenancy who financed the Mission of Ammas that consisted of a Church, rectory, and convent in 1928–1929. He had the confidence of Eugene Cardinal Tisserant, then Cardinal Grand Master, because of charitable assistance to his Diocese in Ostia. Mochi endeavored to revise the Constitution then in effect, which would limit the role of the Latin Patriarch of Jerusalem. However, Mochi retired in 1965 before the proposed change.

In 1966, Cardinal Tisserant announced a new administration of the Order with Nicolo Rizzi, a Swiss, succeeding Mochi as Governor General. On November 19, 1967, a Juridic Commission of the Order prepared a new Constitution that created some difficulties with the Latin Patriarch. A new Presidency was created with Nicolo Rizzi as Governor General, lawyer Mario Latuada as Vice Governor General, and a Monsignor Cazzaniga as Secretary. It was unfortunate that the new Constitution made no mention as to priority of the interest of the Order, which the then Latin Patriarch Beltritti felt was detrimental to the Latin Patriarchate. In April 1968 the Presidency came in a body to Jerusalem and created a commission for programming the works in the Holy Land.

*Count Ludovico Carducci Artenisio,*
*Governor General, Knight of the Collar*

In the beginning of 1969, Rizzi had a slight stroke, resigning his office as Governor General. Pope Paul VI, then reigning Pontiff, appointed Count Castelvetri Cantutti to fill the vacancy. Count Cantutti was a man of high integrity and capability in whom the Holy Father had confidence.

Cardinal Tisserant died in the beginning of 1972 and was succeeded by Cardinal Maximillian de Furstenberg, who was very familiar with the Holy Land since he had been Prefect of the Congregation for the Eastern Churches for five years. Having had experiences in a Patriarchal Archdiocese and acquainted with the Latin Patriarch, his appointment was an excellent one, which subsequent actions and decisions proved.

In October 1976, Prince Paolo Enrico Massimo Lancellotti, a retired Italian diplomat, succeeded Cantutti as Governor General, a venerable man who has proven himself an outstanding leader and who has endeared himself to all the Lieutenants of the Order. The prince has now been appointed Lieutenant General of the Order. His successor is Count Ludovico Carducci Artenisio, a former Italian diplomat.

# CHAPTER 15

# ANCIENT AND PRESENT REQUIREMENTS AND PRIVILEGES OF THE ORDER

In a Papal bull of 1496, Pope Alexander VI included certain requirements of a candidate for insignito to a Knight of the Holy Sepulchre of Jerusalem. These were:

- To be of noble birth
- To take a vow of chastity
- To have sufficient means to honorably support his position as a knight
- To lead an exemplary life
- To be ready to battle the infidel or find a replacement in case of his incapacity to do so
- To participate in the activities of the Priory

However, from 1847 pilgrims were received into the Order as a secular confraternity (not a social fraternity), as distinguished from a religious order in that it had no monastic rule, community of goods, or other essential characteristics of a religious order. Pilgrims were received into the lay confraternity with all the external seriousness and ceremonial format of ancient chivalry. Some were not descendants of the nobility in spite of the fact that nobility was a requirement of knighthood in the Order. Many Knights were not of noble birth as all classes were represented in pilgrimages that entitled them for this honor of chivalry. Subsequently, strict duties that the Knights accepted upon investment included:

- Attendance at daily Mass
- Recitation of five Our Fathers for the Holy Father, the Grand Master, Rulers of Christendom, all Knights and the deceased members of the Order
- Protection of the One, Holy, Apostolic, Catholic Church
- Promotion of peace and justice
- Rejection of sordid gains
- Taking no part in unjust wars
- Leading a model Christian life

# Present Requirements for Admission

Under the present Constitution of the Order approved by Pope Paul VI on July 8, 1977, the requirements for admission are as follows:

- Religious devotion
- Participation in the activities of the Church
- A lay Apostolate, placed at the service of the Church
- *Diligence in the ecumenical spirit,* above all by means of active interest in the well recognized problems in the Holy Land

The Constitution goes on to say:

> The characteristics of the Order consist of its pledge to the Holy Places of Jerusalem and its obligations toward the Church in the Holy Land. It is not possible to stress sufficiently that the charitable work of the Order must have its roots in the spirituality of its Knights and Ladies.

Although not in the Constitution, it has been traditional in the lieutenancies of the United States to observe additional duties and responsibilities of Knights and Ladies of the Order. It is recognized that we are citizens of the most powerful nation on the planet with a unique influence on the events unfolding in the Middle East. American Knights and Ladies speak out as private citizens, not representing the Order or the Church, in support of the Christians of the Holy Land, raising the consciousness of fellow citizens and alerting our representatives to the grave needs of the Christian community in the Holy Land.

A compelling reason for the initiation of the Crusades was the destruction of the Holy Sepulchre. Godfrey de Bouillon and his Knights set out to rectify that desecration and swore their sacred honor and their lives to defend the Holy Sepulchre. Thus, the Order has its roots in the defense of the Holy Sepulchre and continues its reverence today. The defense of the Holy Sepulchre has shifted from warfare to diplomatic efforts. As such, it is an appropriate description of the Knights and Ladies of the Holy Sepulchre that, "They shall reforge their swords into plowshares." Knights and Ladies of the Order follow this prophetic spiritual transformation in our continuing efforts in support of the rights of the Catholic Church in the Holy Land.

The defense of the Holy Sepulchre has been generalized to a defense of all Christian Holy Places in the Holy Land. The outer perimeter of that defense is necessarily the native Christians. A thriving Christian community guarantees the safety and access to living monuments of worship to Our Lord Jesus Christ in the land upon which He walked. Knights and Ladies of the Order of the Holy Sepulchre harken to the historic leadership of the Latin Patriarch of Jerusalem and strive to support the Catholic communities of the Patriarchate. Knights and Ladies also hold a special regard for the Franciscan Custos for his heroic stewardship of the Holy

Places. In this, we recognize the mutual solidarity held by Christians of all denominations and the shared aspirations of our Jewish and Moslem brethren.

## Ancient Privileges of the Knights of the Order

The Guardian of the Custody recorded in a document of 1553 the ancient privileges of the Knights of the Holy Sepulchre that are no longer in effect. These were:

- Powers to legitimatize illegitimate children
- To change a name given in Baptism
- To pardon prisoners they might meet on the way to the scaffold
- To possess goods belonging to the Church even though they were laymen
- To be exempt from all taxes
- To credit notaries
- To cut down a man hanging on a gallows and order for him a decent burial
- To wear brocaded silk garments reserved for Knights
- To enter a Church on horseback
- To fight against the infidel

These were approved by a succession of Popes among whom was Benedict XIV (1740–1758), who for political reasons suppressed an article regarding hostility towards the Muslims. In the same document, it was stated that:*The Order of the Holy Sepulchre of Jerusalem had precedence over all other Orders excepting that of the Golden Fleece.*

## Duties and Responsibilities of Knights and Ladies of the Order

1. Observe and promote the objectives of the Order.

2. Practice the virtue of charity, supporting the Church in the Holy Land.

3. Preserve and propagate the Faith in the Holy Land, aid the religious, cultural, charitable, and social institutions of the Catholic missions, and endeavor to make at least one pilgrimage there.

4. Intensify the practice of the Christian life and evince loyalty to the Pope.

5. Foster in all people of good will an interest in the Holy Places.

6. Set an example as Catholic gentlemen or ladies in word and deeds.

7. Generously support the parish and diocese to which they belong.

8. Participate at meetings and ceremonies of the Order and of the Lieutenancy.

9. Attend the funerals of departed Knights or Ladies.

# CHAPTER 16

# SPECIAL INDULGENCES GRANTED

An indulgence is defined in the Catechism of the Catholic Church as the remission before God of the temporal punishment due sins already forgiven as their guilt is concerned. Spiritual indulgences have been granted to the Equestrian Order of the Holy Sepulchre of Jerusalem by the Supreme Pontiffs. On September 23, 1967, the following was granted the Order by the Apostolic Constitution whereby the revision of Sacred Indulgences was promulgated:

> The Holy Penitentiary, by special and express Apostolic Authority, benignly grants Plenary Indulgences to be acquired by Knights and Ladies of the Equestrian Order of the Holy Sepulchre of Jerusalem with the usual conditions being fulfilled, that is, confession, communion, and prayers for the intentions of the Supreme Pontiff, provided that they make or renew, at least privately the promise of faithfully observing the statutes of their association at the following times:
>
> • On the Day of Investiture
> • On the Feasts of:
>> St. Helena (August 18)
>> St. Pius X (August 21)
>> The Triumph of the Holy Cross (September 14)
>> The Blessed Virgin Mary, Queen of Palestine (October 25)
>
> This is granted at present with the force of "In Perpetuum" in the form of a brief without sending any other Apostolic Letters.

To gain a Plenary Indulgence, it is necessary for a person to be free of all attachment to sin, to perform the work to which the Indulgence is attached, and to fulfill three conditions: 1) Sacramental Confession, 2) Eucharistic Communion, and 3) Prayer for the intentions of the Pope.

The three conditions may be fulfilled several days before or after the performance of the prescribed work, but it is fitting that Communion be received and prayers for the intentions of the Holy Father be offered on the same day the work is performed. The praying for the Pope's intentions will be satisfied by saying one "Our Father" and one "Hail Mary," but the person is free to choose other prayers.

There are several devotional practices for which a Plenary Indulgence is granted:

- Adoration of the Blessed Sacrament for one-half hour
- Devout reading of Sacred Scripture for at least one-half hour
- The Way of the Cross
- The recitation of the Rosary in a church, family group, religious community, or pious association

Only one Plenary Indulgence can be gained in one day, more on the day of death. Indulgences can be applied to the dead by way of suffrage at any Mass. Vatican II has narrowed down the number of Plenary Indulgences to cherish them as something very special, to be approached and gained in a real spirit of appreciation, sacrifice, inner readiness, and disposition.

# CHAPTER 17

# THE HONOR OF INVESTITURE

Investiture into the Equestrian Order of the Holy Sepulchre of Jerusalem cannot be obtained by a candidate through application. A person cannot apply to or join this Order. A Knight or Lady may champion candidates to the Order through a process of ascertainment, invitation, and presentation. In the first step of this process, the champion ascertains whether the candidate meets the requirements of the Order and presents said qualifications to the Lieutenant. This includes the explanation of the history, mission, and functions of the Order to the candidate. Upon his judgment, the Lieutenant invites the candidate to the honor of investiture. If the candidate accepts, he or she must secure a letter of recommendation from their parish pastor. The Lieutenant then presents the candidate for consideration to the Grand Prior of the Lieutenancy. The nomination for investiture comes from the Ordinary of the Diocese to which the candidate belongs. The Holy See will not consider a nomination without an approval letter from the Ordinary. The nomination should be forthcoming in the case of those who have been a source of comfort, aid, or counsel to the Diocesan Ordinary in recognition of that person's best efforts. This offering of investiture is the opportunity to expand those efforts in aiding the Church Universal.

Investiture in the Order, recognized as Ecclesiastic Knighthood, is given to Catholics who are active in Parish and Diocesan work as a labor of love and who have distinguished themselves as an example of faith, motivated by charity and love. It is an honor with responsibility. Knights and Ladies are expected to continue this interest in the work of the Church and be able to contribute to the needs of the Holy Land. To fulfill its mission in obedience to the Holy Father, the Order must have Knights and Ladies who can afford the charity, aid, and financial help required of them to support the Church in the Holy Land. The ideal way to investiture or promotion in the Order is for the local Ordinaries, recognizing the mission of the Order, to nominate worthy Catholics who are able to fulfill the purpose of Ecclesiastic Knighthood supporting the mission of the Equestrian Order of the Holy Sepulchre of Jerusalem.

As in the Age of Chivalry, knighthood is reserved for those strong enough to protect and support others. There are many Apostolates in the Church, and each is geared to a particular purpose with members who are particularly suited to accomplish the work of that mission. One would be insensitive to the feelings of the prospective candidate of any religious group to invite that person when he or she could not assume the obligations imposed. Catholics who are able to fulfill their

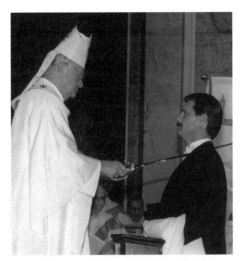

*His eminence James Cardinal Hickey, KGCHS, Grand Prior of the Middle Atlantic Lieutenancy and Archbishop of Washington, DC, administering knighthood in St. Matthew's Cathedral.*

function as Knights and Ladies of the Order are chosen regardless of race or nationality. Knights and Ladies are asked to apply their strength to the mission of the Order in the Holy Land.

Many Bishops in the past have been instrumental in securing certain honors for priests and laymen. It is the tradition in all civilized societies to recognize outstanding merit, distinguished service, and to give some external token of this recognition. Rom. 13:7 says, "One is bound in justice to give honor where honor is due."

Saint Thomas said, "Like the esteem of human glory, honor is good on condition that charity is its principle and the love of God and the love of one's neighbor its object."

His Eminence Edmund Cardinal Szoka has said that it is a mark of distinction to be a Knight or Lady of the Equestrian Order of the Holy Sepulchre of Jerusalem :

> Entering the Order allows a person to become a very real and active participant in a great Catholic tradition. For almost a thousand years, a millennium, the Equestrian Order of the Holy Sepulchre of Jerusalem has continued to foster medieval traditions of chivalry in the midst of an ever changing world.

His Eminence Augustine Cardinal Casaroli, former Papal Secretary of State, has clearly identified one of the essential traits of Knighthood and of our Order:

> As a Knight or Lady of the Equestrian Order of the Holy Sepulchre of Jerusalem is not simply an honor but a calling. Just as Baptism itself brings with it not only the grace of salvation, but also an obligation to live a life of Faith, so to be admitted into this Order of Knighthood is a commitment of Christian services.

Investiture in our Order, an Ecclesiastical Order with all authority in the Holy See, is definitely an honor with responsibility. The Order is important in the life of the Church, which places greater demands on Knights and Ladies of the Equestrian Order of the Holy Sepulchre of Jerusalem, expecting loyalty to the Supreme Pontiff and devotion to the Order's mission in the Holy Land. We must never forget that the Cross we wear is not only an insignia of honor for past services but that we are Knights and Ladies of a living Order dedicated to the fulfillment of specific ideals and to carrying out a definite mission.

On the spiritual side, the Order seeks the development of an "aristocracy" of the soul, of a religious elite who are persuaded that a decent society depends for its survival upon the development in its midst of a spiritual "aristocracy." The Order seeks the development of noblemen and noblewomen in the realm of the divine spirit, of people who are more holy in their personal lives, more loyal to Christ and His Vicar, more generous to Christian causes, and more exemplary in their reflection of the Catholic ideal of personal charities, social action, and religious life. The Order is admittedly "selective" and limits its knighthood to those who have demonstrated that they are in a special way the friends of the missions and Catholic works in the Holy Land. They are special patrons of the Church and the Holy See by their labors or by their generosity.

Knights and Ladies of the Order resolve always to make an impact both on public opinion and on the esteem of the hierarchy without which election to the Order is a pure formality. Knights and Ladies of the Holy Sepulchre realize that the Cross they wear is not only a badge of honor awarded for past service but that they are Knights and Ladies of a living Order dedicated to the fulfillment of specific ideals and to carrying out a definite mission.

We are today confronted with the same challenge as our founding Knights. We must meet the challenge with the same crusading spirit and with the armaments of prayer, example, and charity. To this cause our Order has been and is dedicated. In the light of what is happening in the Holy Land, we have as great and perhaps greater mission to perform as at any time throughout our history. In the words of Pope John Paul II:

> May the honor that comes to you through the Equestrian Order of the Holy Sepulchre of Jerusalem make you feel more and more the burden and the responsibility of distinguishing your toil with an exemplary Christian life and with consistent, generous, and disinterested adherence to Christ and to the Church. In this way you will really enrich your Order with outstanding merits and true glory, and you will give before the world the best confirmation of the reason for its existence and activity.
>
> For my part, in the wake of my venerated predecessors, I stress to you my appreciation and encouragement to continue tirelessly in the beneficial work, which coincides with my solicitude for that Land hallowed by the passing of the Lord and of His Apostles, and towards which my thoughts and my heart turn daily in prayer.
>
> With these sentiments and with these hopes I wish you all success in your commitment and impart to you the conciliatory Apostolic Blessing, which I willingly extend to all Knights and Ladies of your Order.

# CHAPTER 18

# THE CHURCH ON THE HILL

Above the level of the Tiber on the northern slope of the Janiculum Hill stands the fifteenth-century Church of Saint Onofrio. It was on the Feast of Our Lady's Assumption in 1945 that His Holiness Pope Pius XII formally granted the use of the Church dedicated to St. Onofrio as well as the use of the monastery attached to the Church and that part of it occupied by the Museum dedicated to the famous Italian poet, Torquato Tasso, to the Equestrian Order of the Holy Sepulchre of Jerusalem. In the following year the Holy Father entrusted care of the Church to the Franciscan Friars of the Atonement of Graymoor.

The act of His Holiness Pope Pius XII dated August 15,1945, designating the Church of St. Onofrio to be the spiritual center in Rome of the Order of the Holy Sepulchre of Jerusalem, reads as follows:

*Motu Proprio*

The use of the Church dedicated to Saint Onofrio on the Janiculum Hill, together with the adjoining monastery is granted to the Equestrian Order of the Holy Sepulchre of Jerusalem.

Pope Pius XII

Since the Equestrian Order of the Holy Sepulchre of Jerusalem does not have its own Church in the City of Rome, we desire to grant it one which may be not only proof of paternal benevolence towards the Order, but also one that may be especially fitting and have a particular significance for the same.

There is on the Janiculum Hill a splendid Church dedicated to Saint Onofrio, distinguished since the sixteenth century with the honor of being a titular Church of Cardinals belonging to the Order of Priests, this Church appears to us to be most suitable for realizing our desire.

In this Church, in fact, there still lives the memory of Torquato Tasso, illustrious poet, who sang in exquisite verse the deeds of the Crusaders who struggled to restore freedom to the Holy Sepulchre of Jerusalem, and there, too, is an ancient monastery, which—after the legitimate cessation of the Order of Hermits of Jerome—can fittingly accommodate this Equestrian Order of the Holy Sepulchre of Jerusalem and can provide it with a convenient center for the carrying out of its religious ceremonies and its acts of Piety and works of Charity.

Wherefore, after careful consideration of the matter, and having conferred with our dearly beloved son Emanuel Celestine Suhard of Title of Saint Onofrio on the Janiculum, Cardinal Priest of the Holy Roman Church, Archbishop of Paris, by virtue of this Motu Proprio, with certain knowledge and by the fullness of our Apostolic power, we decree and ordain as follows:

1. The use of the Church dedicated to Saint Onofrio on the Janiculum Hill and likewise of the adjoining monastery and the Torquato Tasso Museum with the furnishings and all the property both movable and those things fixed to the soil which are called immovable, is assigned by law to the Equestrian Order of the Holy Sepulchre of Jerusalem;

2. The nomination of the Rector or the other clergy to this Church is the concern of the Sovereign Pontiff having heard the judgment both of the Cardinal Priest of the Title of Saint Onofrio on the Janiculum, and of the Most Eminent Cardinal Vicar of Rome, and of the Most Eminent Cardinal who is Patron of the Equestrian Order of the Holy Sepulchre of Jerusalem at the time;

3. This same Church dedicated to Saint Onofrio shall likewise remain conveniently accessible in the future to all the faithful who may wish to frequent it from a motive of piety;

All of which we have decreed and ordained by the instrument, issued by Motu Proprio, shall be fixed and immutable notwithstanding anything to the contrary, even be it worthy of very special regard.

Given at Rome from St. Peters, August 15, 1945, Feast of the Assumption of the Virgin Mary in the seventh year of our Pontificate.

*Pius XII*

Upon acquisition the Order made extensive repairs and improvements to bring the lovely old church back to its original glory. The ravages of the time had taken their toll, unwise and unartistic remodeling had obscured the simplicity of its lines. Its priceless frescoes had faded over the centuries. The beautiful inner cloister had been refashioned to suit the exigencies of those who had been its occupants.

The Order considered it a sacred trust confided to it to restore and repair the edifice that was to be their own special shrine. The services of qualified artistry and artisans were sought under the chief architect of the Apostolic Palace, Count Enrico Peter Galeazzi who was also the leading layman of the Order. The entire interior of the Church was restored to its former splendor. Stained glass windows bearing the coat-of-arms of the Order replaced the old ones. Richly carved benches of stained oak took the place of wicker chairs and kneelers. In the choir loft alterations were made to provide a place of prayer for the religious community to whom the care and functioning of the Church were later to be entrusted. In the cloister an arduous work of alteration and the delicate task of restoring seventeenth century frescoes were successfully finished in 1947.

The alterations have not resulted in any deviation from the original typical Italian Renaissance style with one nave only. Much of the original Renaissance decorations still remain. Especially notable is the elaborate and colorful apse designed at the beginning of the sixteenth century by Baldassare Peruzzi, one of the most distinguished painters of the times. It richly tells the stories of the New Testament and shows the glory of the sacred personages under the benevolent glance of God, the Father, who blessed them from above. Beneath Him the Angels diffuse harmony, a silent melody of voices and instruments are felt, if not heard. Still lower in the center of the larger fresco is seen the triumphant coronation of the Blessed Virgin Mary. To the sides are groups of Apostles and Sibyls. The paintings in the semicircle are Enthroned Madonna and Child, together with St. John the Baptist, St. Jerome, St. Catherine of Alexandria, and St. Onofrio, the patron of the church. The panels at the left portray the Adoration of the Magi and at the right the Flight into Egypt, with the Slaughter of the Innocents in the background.

The alterations included the enlarging or addition of chapels on both sides of the nave. There are now five spacious chapels in the Church—two on the left side and three on the right side. They are of different merit according to their period and ornamentation. Those on the right are rich with noteworthy works of art. The second chapel on the left was dedicated to Saint Pius X, who during his Pontificate was Grand Master of the Order.

The inner cloister adjoining the Church, designed in the fifteenth century, is another refreshing work of the Renaissance period. It is considered to be one of the quietest and most secluded havens in the City of Rome. The most recent restoration done by the Order in 1946, brought back the upper loggia, which had previously been enclosed. The columns beneath it are of varying styles, having been taken from different ancient buildings.

On the second floor of the Convent at the entrance of Tasso's apartment, there is another treasure, a fresco of the Madonna and Child. The Tasso Museum contains the room in which Tasso spent the last days of his life and where he died. Also, there are several rooms in which are preserved manuscripts, first editions, and translations of the poet's literary works.

The illustrious Tasso, the greatest bard of the Convent of Jerusalem, is buried in the Chapel on the left nearest the entrance. It was also for this reason that Pope Pius XII assigned the church to the Order. It is known that in the spring of 1595, Tasso asked to be brought to the monastery that he might prepare himself for death "with great security and devotion." A short time afterwards, he became seriously ill, and one of his requests was to be buried in the Church of Saint Onofrio.

In the early days the church became dear to the Romans who went to pray and meditate in the secluded spot high above the City of Rome. The church continues to be considered among the most beautiful and most interesting of the smaller churches in Rome. From the garden there is a panoramic view of the majestic City of Rome, with the dome of Saint Peter's Basilica resting above it like a dazzling royal crown.

*The Church of St. Onofrio, Janiculum Hill, Rome*

# CHAPTER 19

# THE INSIGNIA

The beautiful and distinctive insignia of the Equestrian Order of the Holy Sepulchre of Jerusalem utilizes the Cross Potent between four crosslets of the Kingdom of Jerusalem, but while the arms of Jerusalem are gold on a silver field, the Cross of the Order is red. This design has been attributed to Godfrey de Bouillon, but the likelihood that he ever bore these arms is very slight. In point of fact the period of the first crusade effectively predated the development of ancient and more modern heraldry as we know it. The crusades may, indeed, have provided a strong impetus for the development of hereditary armorial bearings, but Princess Anna Comnena of Byzantium, who chronicled the activities of the Crusaders in Constantinople, stated that the shields of the crusaders were blank of formal coat of arms. Sometimes shields were cameoed by an animal. The most recognized was a lion adopted by the Plantagenets, the family name of the Angevin line of English sovereigns from Henry II [1154] through Richard III [1485].

The Matthew Paris roll of arms (c.1280) identified the arms of Godfrey de Bouillon as a plain silver cross on a gold field. It must again be questioned whether or not he bore these arms, or if they might not more likely be the creation of a later herald. The familiar cross potent first appears in the Walford roll (c.1475) as the principal charge of the "Roi d'Acre." It was a gold cross potent on a silver field sprinkled with many small crosses. This was subsequently modified to the design with which we are familiar.

It has been suggested that the original insignia of the Order was a patriarchal cross with double bar, and that sometime following the fall of Acre in 1291, the insignia assumed the more familiar shape that we know today. This contention is supported by Sir William Segar, whose book *Honor, Military and Civil*, published in 1602, described the Cross of the Order as following the patriarchal form. It is certain in any case that the insignia of the separate national jurisdictions varied prior to the rebirth of the order in 1847. For instance, the French jurisdiction used the cross potent with fleurs-de-lis between the arms of the cross, and a central boss portraying the risen Christ.

Today the five-fold Cross of the Order is worn pendant from the military trophy authorized by Pope Saint Pius X. The fundamental rank of all Confreres and Consoeurs of the Order is that of Knight or Lady, as has always been the case with the ancient Orders. Indeed, certain great Orders still consist of that single grade. At present, however, most Orders divide their knights into three to five grades, while the Equestrian Order of the Holy Sepulchre of Jerusalem has four: Knight (KHS); Commander (KCHS); Commander with Star, which in international practice is usually termed a "Grand Officer" and so termed in the Constitution of 1977 (KC*HS); and Grand Cross (KGCHS). The insignia of the Knights was previously worn on the left breast, but is now conferred on a necklet, the Commanders in a larger size on a necklet, the Commanders with Star on a necklet with the addition of an octagonal silver star worn on the left side, and the knights of the Grand Cross wear the insignia resting on the left hip, pendant from a sash that passes over the right shoulder, and a star on the left side of a formal black jacket. The insignia itself differs only in size for the different grades. The ribbon (riband) of the Order is of black watered silk. Ladies of the Order display the same insignia as the Knights but without the military trophy, suspending the Cross from a gold bow.

There are in addition a very limited number of Knights and Ladies of the Collar. The Collar consists of Crosses of the Order alternating with rectangular gold plaques with the motto "Deus Lo Vult" from which hangs the military trophy and the Cross of the Order, surmounted by the gold figure of Christ rising from the Sepulchre and surrounded by a garland of leaves in gold and enamel.

While the Order possesses an elaborate white uniform, this is not used in the American Lieutenancies, and the insignia is worn instead with formal civilian dress. On select occasions the white cape of the Order, authorized by Pope Saint Pius X, is worn by the Knights, while the Ladies wear a black mantle with the Cross of the Order on the left side.

A traditional method of displaying knighthood in an Order of Chivalry has for centuries been to attach the insignia of the Order to the Knights' or Ladies' coat of arms. Certain recognized international forms prevail in this, and the Equestrian Order of the Holy Sepulchre of Jerusalem has outlined these regulations in its Constitution. That document states:

- Knights and Ladies may suspend the Cross of the Order under the point of the shield "with a black knot"
- Commanders may suspend the insignia from "a black ribbon limited to the base of the shield"
- Commanders with Star may suspend the insignia "with trophy suspended from a black ribbon rising from the sides of the shield"
- Knights and Ladies of the Grand Cross "bind the shield with the ribbon of the Order, from which hangs the Cross with trophy"

Knights and Ladies of the Collar and Grand Cross, members of the Grand Magisterium, Lieutenants, and Grand Priors may quarter the arms of the Order on the same shield as their own coat of arms, with the Cross of the Order in the first and fourth quarters.

The principal insignia of the Order is its ancient and beautiful five-fold cross, the Cross of the Five Wounds. This consists of a central cross, surrounded by four smaller crosses, traditionally said to symbolize the "five most precious wounds of

Christ." It has for centuries been symbolic of the Holy City of Jerusalem itself. It indicates honor and devotion to the Order of the Holy Sepulchre of Jerusalem.

The cross, as used by the Order, is in red enamel, bordered in gold. It is made in various sizes to identify rank, and when used for Knights it is surmounted by a military trophy, whose use was decreed by Pope Saint Pius X, the Grand Master of the Order, to distinguish Knights' insignia from Ladies'. The Ladies of the Holy Sepulchre of Jerusalem had been created by Pius' predecessor, Pope Leo XIII. The Ladies' cross is surmounted by a knotted bow in gold. All crosses of the Order are suspended from black moire silk ribbons of various widths, and are worn in the manner described below.

## KNIGHTS

*Knights of the Grand Cross* wear a large cross and military trophy suspended from a wide black sash or baldric which is placed over the right shoulder, crossing the breast and back diagonally and ending at the left hip. A large eight-pointed or rayed silver star of rank, charged with a large cross, is also worn low on the left breast of a formal black coat.

*Commanders with Star* wear a medium cross and military trophy around the neck, suspended from a black ribbon of medium width. A large eight-pointed or rayed silver star of rank, charged with a small cross surrounded by a golden circle bearing a green laurel wreath, is also worn low on the left breast of a formal black coat.

*Commanders* wear the medium cross and military trophy suspended from a modest width black ribbon around the neck.

*Knights* wear a small cross and military trophy on a narrow black ribbon around the neck. Alternately, Knights may wear the old badge-type insignia, like a medal on the left breast of the coat. This is still a valid and traditional insignia, but it has been replaced by the neck ribbon style for ease in placement during the investiture ceremony.

It is appropriate to bear the miniature decoration either with the full-size insignia, or alone, on both full evening dress (white tie) and dinner jackets (black tie). This miniature is a yellow and white gold papal bar of small size from which hangs a black silk ribbon and a miniature of the cross or star of appropriate rank. These may be worn on any social occasion.

It is not considered to be socially acceptable to wear a limited number of full-size insignia with dinner jackets (black tie). One neck insignia and a single star may be worn, while the number of miniatures is not limited. The Grand Cross sash is not appropriate for any but full evening dress (white tie). Proper protocol requires the riband to be worn under the white vest unless the person is a diplomat of high rank and is an active representative of his government. The riband is worn over the vest in the presence of a head of government, the Pope, and the Grand Master of the Order.

Neither full-size insignia nor miniatures are appropriate for wear with business suits or daytime attire. However, there is a small, flat lapel badge, or, alternately, a rosette, both of which display a small Cross of the Order and an indication of rank. Knights are encouraged to wear these on dignified business suits at all times as it invites questions concerning the Order. Be prepared to proffer a characterization of the Order, an explanation of our mission, and a declaration of our spiritual fidelity to the Supreme Pontiff.

## LADIES

*Ladies of the Grand Cross* wear an insignia of rank in the same manner and of the same size as Knights of the Grand Cross. The only difference is that the Grand Cross insignia for Ladies has a gold bow in place of the military trophy.

*Lady Commanders with Star* normally wear their insignia about the neck, with the star pinned to the left side. However, due to the fact that the star is very heavy and difficult to pin to certain fabrics, it is supplied with a black silk ribbon to which it may be attached and worn about the neck. In which case the neck-cross is not worn.

*Ladies and Lady Commanders* wear the cross of their rank on a necklet, in the appropriate smaller size, unless they possess the older badge that is then worn pinned to the upper left side of the dress.

For social daytime or evening wear, Ladies of the Order are permitted to detach their proper cross of rank from its ribbon, and wear it hung from a gold chain or in other appropriate fashion. They may also wear their miniatures with dignified evening dress, and their emblem stickpins at any time.

## OTHER INSIGNIA

Other insignia validly awarded to a Knight or Lady for military or governmental service by either a foreign government, or other authentic Orders of Chivalry, may be worn with the emblem of the Order of the Holy Sepulchre of Jerusalem. If there are many, they may be worn in miniature, or only the most important ones should be selected. Miniatures may be arranged from right to left in decreasing order of rank, or in order of award with the most recent to the left. No more than four different insignia are worn to conform with accepted heraldic etiquette.

## CLERGY INSIGNIA

During ceremonies Priest-Knights may wear insignia of rank on their mozzettas, either in the badge form on the left breast or about the neck. For formal occasions full insignia are properly worn on a cassock of appropriate color according to ecclesiastical rank. The baldric and star of the Grand Cross are worn over the cassock. The star of the Commander with Star is worn on the left side of the cassock above the waist. At formal banquets or receptions of the Order, clergy knights are encouraged to wear their insignia in keeping with the formal dress of the other Knights. The regulations for clergy uniforms and/or insignia may be modified by the direction of the Grand Prior.

## THE PILGRIM SHELL

The Pilgrim Shell is the choicest emblem of the Order and is awarded by the Latin Patriarch of Jerusalem. This medallion consists of a scallop shell, the ancient badge of a pilgrim, in oxidized silver. In the center is placed the Cross of the Order in red fired enamel bordered with gold. It is usually worn with evening dress. It is placed above all other religious and secular insignia. It is the only insignia that may be worn on the outside of either the Lady's or Knight's cape.

The Pilgrim Shell can be earned by any Knight or Lady of the Order in good standing, who makes a pious pilgrimage to Jerusalem and prays at the Holy Sepulchre of our Risen Lord. Knights and Ladies of the Order who are planning private pilgrimages to the Holy Land should request in advance that the Lieutenant make arrangements for having the Pilgrim Shell awarded to them.

It is customary for those who possess the Pilgrim Shell to wear it at all times with any dress during the entire two days of the annual meeting. It is also appropriate to wear it at any meeting of the Order. One Lieutenancy has also authorized a specially designed blazer patch, incorporating the Pilgrim Shell, the Patriarch's cross and Shield, and the motto of the Order, "Deus Lo Vult," hand embroidered in silver and red.

## AWARDS OF MERIT

The constitution of the Order provides the awarding of honors to persons of unquestionable moral conduct in recognition of particular meritorious charity in the Holy Land. Such persons do not need to assume responsibilities imposed on Knights and Ladies. The recipients do not receive the title of Knight or Lady of the Order.

Insignia of Merit are of three classes:Cross of Merit; Cross of Merit with Silver Star; and Cross of Merit with Gold Star. Merit emblems are worn similar to those insignia bestowed upon Knights and Ladies of the Order of the Holy Sepulchre of Jerusalem. No capes are worn.

# CHAPTER 20

# UNIFORM REGULATIONS

In former years Knights and Matrons [Ladies, Dames] had ornate formal hand-made uniforms. This formal dress was abolished by Pope Paul VI.

## KNIGHTS

Knights of the American Lieutenancies of the Order wear a ceremonial uniform comprised of a cape and beret. The cape is of white ivory cloth, full cut, reaching to approximately half-way between the knee and ankle, with a short, turned over collar of white velvet secured at the neck. The cape bears the Cross of the Order in scarlet cloth on the left breast below the shoulder. There is no other closure, and the cape hangs somewhat open from the collar closure down.

The beret is of black velvet and has a large, soft, draping crown. The head band is also covered with black velvet, and is raised upward on the right front side to a height of 12 cm. On this raised portion is a patch indicating rank: for Knights, a cross on a shield of silver braid; Commander, one circle with gold braid; Commander with Star, two circles of gold braid; Knights of the Grand Cross, the shield encircled with a garland of olive leaves embroidered in gold and a single circle of gold braid. The beret is worn with the emblem of rank on the right forehead midway between the eye and ear. The crown is given a little tug to the opposite side to seat the beret properly upon the head.

The cape and beret are worn at all ceremonies, indoors and out, when requested by the Lieutenant or Grand Prior. During Mass, the beret is removed only at the beginning of the Eucharistic Prayer and is replaced after the ablutions. A convenient reminder for the doffing and replacing of the beret is the time when such bishops as are in attendance, or celebrating, remove and replace their zucchettos.

For very formal ceremonial occasions the cape would be worn over full evening dress (white tie), with full insignia on the coat. On less formal occasions the cape may be worn over dinner jackets (black tie), or over a simple dark suit when so specified by the Lieutenant. For all occasions notification of the type of dress required will be made prior to the date of the ceremony. Casual or sporting type clothing or shoes are never appropriate on any occasion when the cape is to be worn.

## LADIES

Ladies of the Order wear a full-cut, ankle length black cape that may be of velvet or satin. The cape has a short self collar, usually worn upright. It is fastened at the throat by a tie or frog of black silk braid. The Order's cross, in scarlet cloth, is placed on the left breast of the cape below the shoulder. The cape is worn over a long black dress for formal occasions, such as investiture ceremonies, with black gloves that may be long or short depending on the sleeve length of the dress. When wearing the cape, the head is always covered with a black veil or mantilla. For informal ceremonies the cape may be worn over a short or long dress, with dark, preferably black, shoes.

## RANK

Knights and Ladies do not wear the insignia of rank or other decorations on the outside of the cape, with the sole exception of the Pilgrim Shell. Tradition holds that this most important emblem may be worn by those Knights and Ladies who have earned it, on the outside of the cape, centered on the Cross of the Order. Unauthorized, unearned use of the Pilgrim Shell is strictly forbidden.

## CAPES

The capes of the Order are religious vestments and are intended solely for use at religious ceremonies at which the Order or individual Knights and Ladies have been asked to participate. They are not to be worn in public functions and ceremonies without prior permission of the Lieutenant or Grand Prior.

## CAPES OF DIGNITARIES

The Lieutenant General, Governor General, Vice Governors General, Members of the Grand Magisterium, and Lieutenants in office, or Honorary Lieutenants, have the privilege of wearing the Capitular Cape. This cape is of white cloth, very full and flowing, reaching to the ground. It has a large, turned-out collar of white velvet, and is completely closed in front. It carries the Order's Cross on the left breast below the shoulder as on the Knight's cape. Worn over the Capitular Cape is a heavy braided gold cord with two large gold tassels in front, carrying two sliding clasps, one in front and one in back.

## CLERGY KNIGHTS

Priest-Knights of the Order have the privilege of wearing the long white cape exactly as do the lay Knights. However, at the present time the mozzetta is more commonly worn. This is a short, white cape, closed in the front by covered buttons, having a short standing collar. The mozzetta is worn over a cassock, and, if desired, a rochet with black cuffs, unless by another title their proper cuffs are of violet or crimson.

Priest-Knights may and should wear their insignia of rank, and any other proper decoration, around the neck or on the left breast. If the long white cape is worn, the decorations may be worn on the cassock.

# III

## Ideal Chivalry

*Such was Godfredo's countenance, such his cheer,*
*That from his eye sure conquest flames and streams,*
*Heaven's gracious favors in his looks appear,*
*And great and goodly more than erst he seems;*
*His face and forehead full of nobless were,*
*And on his cheek smiled youth's purple beams,*
*And in his gait, his grace, his acts, his eyes,*
*Somewhat far more than mortal, lives and lies.*

*Jerusalem Delivered* by Torquato Tasso (1544–1595)
translated by Edward Fairfax (1560–1635)
Twentieth Book, Stanza VII

# CHAPTER 21

# THE CODE OF CHIVALRY

The Code of Chivalry was developed as a morally binding code of behavior for a unique ruling class composed of equestrian warriors expert in heavy cavalry techniques. This code was a direct result of the efforts of the Roman Catholic Church to civilize and redeem a barbarian Europe and the warriors who ruled. The period of chivalric molding bloomed in the latter part of the eleventh century along with the call to the Crusades. Thus the Code of Chivalry is directly linked to the crusading spirit of Christianity.

There were many interpretations of chivalry, some displaying various degrees of civil refinement and spiritual salvation as well as those regressing to a time of pre-Christian darkness. The Code of Chivalry was enforced when there was a severe tension between the forces of life and those of death. The business of warfare reflected the barbaric roots from which the societies recently emerged. War was an extremely physical challenge with the will to dominate being an important factor in overcoming personal exhaustion and fear. The separation between life and death, physical and the spiritual, was measured by the edge of the broadsword. It was in this manner that the battle of good against evil was fought. The battle was joined when evil forces from the East threatened genocide and the destruction of Christianity. The Code of Chivalry was developed as a behavioral roadmap used to mold the warrior class to become benevolent stewards of Christendom and resolute defenders of the people of God. A just governance based on this code was to be accomplished with social graces and within the framework of charitable love.

The bond of the code was the knight's personal relationship to God, which was reinforced by the frequent excursions in battle, facing death, in defense of the Faith. Besides the development of war skills, chivalry included meditation on the Five Wounds of Christ and the embrace of the chivalric virtues. When knights accepted the Cross in the Crusades, the impact of the Five Wounds of Christ weighed heavily on mind and heart. The dedicated religious warrior also acceded to the chivalric virtues. Thus was the character of the defenders of the Christian faith, from which the Knights and Ladies of the Equestrian Order of the Holy Sepulchre of Jerusalem are spiritually descended.

The Code of Chivalry is living and well. It should influence modern leaders and all those of good heart. Today, we do not look at nobility as a birthright. Its original meaning "to be recognized" is consonant with the Catholic Church's dubbing Knights and investing Ladies. The Chivalric Virtues are Gentilesse, Charité,

Courtoisie, Loyauté, and Largesse.

These virtues are overlaid on the Cross with the Five Wounds, the insignia of the Equestrian Order of the Holy Sepulchre of Jerusalem. Coincident with the Cross Potent is the central virtue of Gentilesse. The upper right crosslet is Charité. It is the strong right arm of the chivalric virtues and is balanced by that of the upper left, Courtoisie. The lower right, Loyauté is is balanced by the lower left, Largesse.

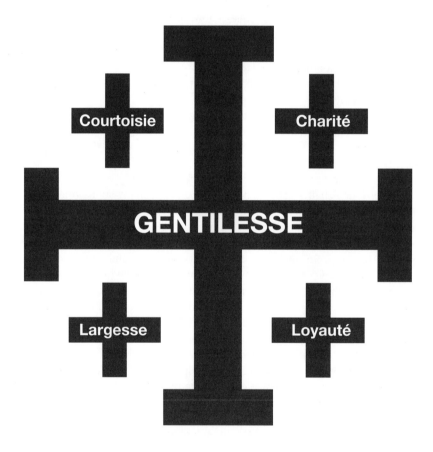

# CHAPTER 22

# GENTILESSE

In the depth of the Dark Ages, the supreme warrior was epitomized by the beserker, one who developed a war rage. Seeming to float on the energy of egocentric experience, he attacked totally without regard to his personal well-being. A new warrior then arose: one who could stand outside the boundaries of his own limitations, and fight on forever in the mind of his opponent. This new chivalric warrior was molded by the virtue of Gentilesse. This virtue was central to his supremacy. Its development is seen today as reflected in the grueling and often insulting training in the armed forces. Gentilesse is the ability to suspend the reaction of rage, to calm the spirit, and to deal effectively with reality as it exists. It includes leaving the egocentricity of oneself, and becoming open to evaluate the external objective world. Through that knowledge, the chivalrous knights became supreme on the battlefield, effectively encountering their opponents while trying to avoid precipitate and ungallant tactics.

Gentilesse was molded during civil pastimes, making the formerly unbearable barbaric warrior a socially acceptable person. A gentleness became the hallmark in both civil attitude and in the application of power. This virtue was so highly regarded that the entire ruling class chose to be identified with it as the "gentility."

The transcendent foundation of Gentilesse lies in the second Beatitude. In the words of Saint Sir Ignatius of Loyola, as interpreted by Fr. John Harden, meekness as Christ lives it is the effective control of the passion of anger. However, the term meekness does not fully translate the full meaning of the Greek of St. Matthew. Gentleness is also a valid translation. Thus, an understandable and accurate translation of the Second Beatitude is, "Blessed are the gentle." Moreover, this gentleness is the same gentleness that Christ exercises. Only the strong can be gentle. Gentleness is to be employed in our loving exercise of strength.

Christ's dialogue of the Beatitudes is a description of Himself. This comes to quite a surprise to many, never having considered Christ as meek in any manner. Christ is the strongest of all human beings to walk this planet. With this in mind, Pope John Paul II reminds us in his encyclical letter, *Veritatis Splendor:*

> The Beatitudes are not specifically concerned with certain particular rules of behavior. Rather, they speak of basic attitudes and dispositions in life, and therefore they "do not coincide exactly with the Commandments." On the other hand, "there is no separation or opposi-

tion" between the Beatitudes and the Commandments: both refer to the good, to eternal life. The Sermon on the Mount begins with the proclamation of the Beatitudes, but also refers to the Commandments. At the same time, the Sermon on the Mount demonstrates the openness of the Commandments and their orientation towards the horizon of the perfection proper to the Beatitudes. These latter are above all "promises," from which there also indirectly flow "normative indications" for the moral life. In their originality and profundity they are a sort of "self-portrait of Christ," and for this very reason are "invitations to discipleship and to communion of life with Christ."

"Meekness," says Fr. Harden on the thoughts of St. Ignatius, "is a virtue of temperance." With it we learn to control "our spontaneous tendency to anger when we are opposed or contradicted or... if something or someone... stands in our way. Meekness masters irascibility. Gentleness... is a virtue of charity which loves the persons over whom we have power." Consider the combination "to have power over people and to love them" while never flaunting one's dominance over them, be it "political, or financial," or social. Gentilesse is the kindly exercise of power. Gentilesse demands that the powerful must respect those over whom they have power. The powerless are our benefactors because it is by loving them that we prove and show our love for God.

With Gentilesse, we gain an "influence over the hearts of others in direct proportion to the measure of our gentleness." This is what Christ meant by, "They shall possess the Earth." He certainly did not mean things of the material. His concern is not of things but of the people of God. It is over these beloved of Christ that Gentilesse has its profound effect. Thus it is easy to see the primary value of Gentilesse in the system of chivalric virtues. It is at the very center of noblesse. It is the center around which subordinate virtues orient.

# CHAPTER 23

# CHARITÉ

The chivalrous knight was trained intensely to acquire superlative equestrian combat skills. Much of the training was based on the knight's desire to excel and hinged on his self-reliance, self-motivation, and self-direction. These determinations were brought by the knight to his training. Those not so inclined were quickly discarded by their lords or removed by the competitive selection of mortal combat.

The chivalrous knight cared deeply about his activities. Nothing was worth doing without a passionate zest for life. The knight cared for the wholeness of life in all its physical and spiritual dimensions. His gaze was never dimmed by a segregation of secular and religious thoughts. The knight recognized the great extent of God's gifts everywhere. He recognized God's personal interaction with his own experience. His fortune or misfortune in war, life, and love critically depended upon his personal relationship with Our Lord, Jesus Christ.

With this insight and zest, the chivalrous knight went on quests, seeking out injustices in all their manifestations, then fought to overturn them. The knight swore to uphold the will of God, taking oaths only in the most somber fashion, and never to break his word. These knights heard the great call of Pope Urban II to defend Christendom, took the cross, and set off on the heroic Crusades.

There were times when the knight was overwrought by the intensity of medieval life, and consequently separated himself in a personal retreat to reflect upon God. The knight would seek the Holy Grail in a gradual process of growing in Christ over one's lifetime. The knight would find a holy hermit to assist him in discovering God's graces and in building the peace and strength that comes only from Our Lord. The chivalrous knight devoutly drank the Blood of Christ from the Chalice of Life. The strength drawn from the Holy Blood is the true charger upon which the virtue of Charité is carried within the chivalrous knight and lady. The penitent knight enters into a personal relationship with Christ, into a Holy Communion that extends into the spiritual dimensions with a detachment from the physical that purges the soul.

Charité is the knight's and lady's ability to care with an intensity and commitment, and is applied in three directions: towards Our Lord, towards the people of God, and towards one's own personal activities. As said in Revelation 3:

> I know all about you: how you are neither cold nor hot.
> I wish you were one or the other, but since you are neither, but only luke-warm, I will spit you out of my mouth.

Christ wants intensity and commitment from us: ponder His level of sacrifice and commitment. Meditate on His Five Wounds and take up the Cross.

Charité towards the people of God takes a specific direction for the strong. The knight and lady must use their strengths for those in need, for the downtrodden, for those who suffer injustice. The old word for this direction of Charité is *Pitie*. One must be able to have pity on another human being, and be moved to action. The knights did not stand aside and consider the legal ramifications and whether to get involved. Their Charité generated a boldness that drove them to overcome seemingly insurmountable obstacles. They had pity for the unfortunate and moved to relieve the injustice. This is a major characteristic sought by the Knights and Ladies of the Order of the Holy Sepulchre of Jerusalem, who must be strong enough to defend others. The Order looks for those strong enough to stand up against the bigotries hurled at the Catholic Church, to stand by the deserted, to protect the weak, to feed the hungry, and to care for the diseased and aged. Such heroes and heroines are the ones who manifest their strength in Christ. These are the ones sought who are offered the Cross, and invited to broaden their mission to include the Christians of the Holy Land. They are on the ground in the Holy Land, directly helping the Latin Patriarch, the Custos, the people under their care, and preserving the Holy Places of Christian reverence. There are many more who support these by spreading the cape of advocacy over them in prayer and philanthropy. The transcendent foundation of knightly charity lies in the Fourth Beatitude, "Blessed are those who hunger and thirst for justice."

The emotions of hunger and thirst are most basic for survival. When food or water supplies are threatened, we react with extreme emotions. This intensity is what Christ is asking of us: an intense desire to see that justice is done; that we respond and act when confronted by injustice. It takes Charité, with each of us actively moving to correct injustices. And how will we recognize an injustice? It is simple: by recognizing that which is opposed to the Will of God. The fundamental spiritual conflict is the will of man against the Will of God. Recognizing what is right, what is consistent with God's plan, the chivalrous Knight and Lady move into action.

Literature is filled with tales of knights venturing forth into an inhospitable land where rogue warriors terrorized the God-fearing. The domains between the realms were lawless, and many a warlord who had not yet converted to chivalry readily exploited the weak. Hearing the cries of the afflicted, the chivalrous knight directed his war talents to bring relief and justice to those he met along the way of questing. The chivalrous knight achieved heroic feats in the name of Our Lord, Jesus Christ, thus receiving the remuneration of the Fourth Beatitude, "For they shall be satisfied."

In this errand the knight had pity on the afflicted, becoming a champion of the people of God in the earthly realm of God. Given that the entire culture was Christian, chivalrous knights became renowned and highly regarded in their own time as Christ's Champions. If the knight became too intense with the material world, however, he risked losing sight of Charité and his behavior could become tyrannical. As a check on this possibility, the chivalrous knight was to cultivate *Courtoisie*.

# CHAPTER 24

# COURTOISIE

Two knights face each other across an open field. The conflicts between realms has brought them to this confrontation. Helmets on, they hold their lances in the ready position. Leaning forward, their horses sense the shift in weight, feel the light touch of the spurs, and recognize the command to charge. They leap forward, straining under their armor, and hurl their bodies against each other. Just before impact, knights lower their lances. The collision dents their shields and nearly unhorses a combatant. Regaining his balance while turning his steed, he calls out and compliments the opponent, "That was quite an excellent try. You nearly unhorsed me!" The opponent, equally chivalrous, returns the compliment.

Here two mortal enemies show Courtoisie under the extreme tension of battle. To be able to do this, the chivalrous knight had to practice the arts of compliment in much less stressful daily living. This practice became a discipline that checked the brutal passions.

Courtoisie has been called the art of gracious living. It is the most obvious mark of a chivalrous knight and a lady. It includes a cheerful engagement of life and the ready response to others through the courtesy of friendly greetings. Courtoisie reflects an openness in the knight and lady for civil and gracious social interaction. Conversation is conducted with ease and sincerity. True compliments are paid while avoiding pomposity, lies, deceit or flattery. It is an overt characteristic that can be mastered by all through the willing application of compliments appropriate to the circumstances.

Courtoisie defuses stress arising from inadvertent opposition. A simple and gracious "pardon me" allows another to accept an unintended slight. Daily living gives rise to many situations where Courtoisie can be applied: from moving the car out of the way of a neighbor's access, to rendering simple favors to business associates, or to lending a hand to one's spouse or child. In doing so the knight and lady maintains a sense of humility. From such a position, one's eyes are opened to beauty in others, in the patterns of life, and in the patterns of creation.

Courtoisie requires the avoidance of rash judgment. When a judgment cannot be made by the knight or lady, St. Sir Ignatius of Loyola helps clarify the next step, careful to interpret insofar as possible his neighbor's thoughts, words, and deeds in a favorable way:

Let him ask how the other understands it. And if the latter understands it badly, let the former correct him with love. If that does not suffice, let the Christian try all suitable ways to bring the other to a correct interpretation so that he may be saved.

Courtoisie resonates with Gentilesse, where the powerful never flaunt their dominance over those entrusted by God to their care. Power and strength are sacred gifts, not to be abused. The physical tendency of the powerful to misuse their positions must be countered at all possible opportunities. This includes the avoidance of rude, crude, or barbaric behavior. Courtoisie demands a polished set of manners with a high moral standard. Godfrey de Bouillon was a model of such Courtoisie. He was considered to be one of the most chivalrous knights of the First Crusade. The other knights readily acknowledged him and accepted him as their overlord, due to his exemplary Courtoisie as well as his martial skills.

Courtoisie is practiced among the Knights and Ladies of the Equestrian Order of the Holy Sepulchre of Jerusalem in a manner that eliminates all traces of classism. They are not separated from the people of God, but rather strive to become their champions and servants. Regardless of their fortunes or stations in life, they form a great fellowship and are engaged in a common mission to support the Christians in the Holy Land and to preserve the Sacred Places. The Knights and Ladies' stature is solely in the Lord. They have the Courtoisie to acknowledge this fact with appropriate humility. The words of Nicholas Cardinal Canali express this modesty:

No vain and empty pride of decorations and uniforms—however honorable and meritorious they may be—should flatter with its allure those whom the Supreme Pontiff honors with the name of Crusaders. The only legitimate pride is that which the ardent Apostle of the Gentiles inculcated among the Galatians: God forbid I should glory save in the Cross of Our Lord Jesus Christ. The one boast we may make is that of being and of proving ourselves, in the sight of God and man, truly militant under the Standard of the Risen Christ, Who, upon the empty Sepulchre, vanquishes death, and raises aloft the Crusading Banner of Salvation, of Life and Resurrection.

# CHAPTER 25

# LOYAUTÉ

As Charité and Courtoisie form the virtuous right and left arms of a Knight and Lady, Loyauté and Largesse form the foundation upon which they stand up to the winds of this world. Loyauté is above all else the virtue of being true to Our Lord, Jesus Christ. He is acknowledged as Our Lord and Savior, and Knights and Ladies of the Equestrian Order of the Holy Sepulchre of Jerusalem strive to make clear the path of His second coming and the direct rule of God upon the Earth. They don't mince words when it comes to their relationship with God. They are Christian soldiers and prayer-warriors, striving to emulate Our Lord, and shouldering a unique mission in the Holy Land.

Remembering Our Lord's words, "Give unto God the things that are God's," they acknowledge that Loyauté is being spiritually loyal to the Vicar of Jesus Christ, in their obedience to the Supreme Pontiff. The Order represents the Holy See and is included in the *Annuario Pontifico.* Knights and Ladies pledge to him their devotion and take to heart and prayer all his concerns. Loyalty to the Pope directly complements their activities in the Holy Land. Their loyalty moves upward through the Lieutenants and the Grand Priors to the Grand Magisterium in Rome.

Loyauté is keeping the one true faith, and rising to the defense of the Roman Catholic Church whenever and wherever it is attacked. Through the insightful instruction of our Pope, the Order recognizes an ecumenical relationship in Christ with all Christian Churches, as well as the goodness of our elder brothers in faith, our Jewish associates. The Order perpetuates an association with Islam in the shared worship of the "one God, living and subsistent, merciful and omnipotent, the Creator of Heaven and Earth."

Loyauté requires that a Knight and Lady maintain respect and give honor to their parents as stated in the Fourth Commandment, "Honor thy father and thy mother." Honor extends to their siblings, their spouses, and to their children. The chivalrous Knight and Lady maintain chaste and romantic family relationships regardless of the challenges and difficulties presented in this world. The children born of such a blessed union are raised in an atmosphere of mutual respect, love, honor, and fear of the Lord, Our God.

Honor is a key to chivalry, and is not to be confused with pride. "Honor is the social witness given to human dignity."[1] It follows that a Knight and Lady remain

---

1. Catechism of the Catholic Church, Article 2479

loyal to the Order, upholding its dignity in all social contexts. Care is taken to assure that their deportment, social actions, and spoken words are beyond reproach.

Loyauté requires self-integrity. Such integrity includes holding one's word sacred as one holds one's faith immutable. Knights and Ladies respect that they are Temples of the Holy Spirit. Confident in their spiritual fulfillment, they turn to the physical world in further application of their fidelity. Expressed in the words of Our Lord, "Give unto Caesar the things that are Caesar's," Loyauté requires fidelity to our nation, supporting its society in its journey to God, its economics in providing for the general welfare, and its defense in assuring our mutual freedoms. In the words of Pope Pius XI, our loyalties are to be directed by the principle of subsidiarity so that:

> a community of a higher order should not interfere in the internal life of a community of a lower order, depriving the latter of its functions, but rather should support it in case of need and help to coordinate its activity with the activities of the rest of society, always with a view to the common good.

According to the Catechism of the Catholic Church:

> God has not willed to reserve to himself all exercise of power. He entrusts to every creature the functions it is capable of performing, according to the capacities of its own nature. This mode of governance ought to be followed in social life. The way God acts in governing the world, which bears witness to such great regard for human freedom, should inspire the wisdom of those who govern human communities. They should behave as ministers of divine providence.[2]

---

2. Catechism of the Catholic Church, Article 1884

# CHAPTER 26

# LARGESSE

Largesse is the virtue of giving with an unselfish generosity. It proceeds from a greatness of spirit underlying a nonchalant, impartial (not to be confused with care-less) attitude toward money and wealth. It is sacrificial in that it defines giving from substance rather than surplus. Largesse is a response to the movement of the Holy Spirit as the Spirit places exigent challenges along life's path.

Largesse is best shown by recalling the following examples as actually per-formed by Knights and Ladies of the Equestrian Order of the Holy Sepulchre of Jerusalem:

1. Assessing the exigent housing needs of native Christians in the Holy Land, a great Lady graciously covers the expense of building three housing units on Franciscan land. The Franciscans are doubly happy since they must use their historic lands for immediate community benefit or lose them through govern-ment seizure.

2. Noticing a large man quickly moving through garbage while picking scraps of food, eating and moving on, a humble knight, noble of heart, quickly assesses the situation, immediately approaches the man, and places enough money in his hand for a good meal.

3. After having listened to the Holy Father advise the faithful to be prepared to look for Christ in those at the margins of society, a loyal knight comes upon a mother and child, obviously foreign to Rome, in need of medicine for the child. He opened his wallet and gave half of all that he had to the mother.

4. Coming upon a stranded priest in the Holy Land, a compassionate Knight writes a check to pay for the priest's passage back to Rome. Moreover, the knight covers the next year's educational expenses of the young priest, who was a student at the Pontifical Bible Institute.

5. Knowing a young native American cowboy could not afford his gear for employment, a benevolent knight presents him with a horse, saddle, and bri-dle.

6. Listening to a poorly dressed but powerful man fail in his attempt to elicit a meal from a fearful and cautious cashier at a delicatessen, a sympathetic

knight directly approaches the two saying in an affable manner "I'll pay for whatever this good man chooses to eat."

7. A dedicated knight helped to found a Catholic Medical School and Hospital in Rome. Not only did he give a substantial amount of his own wealth, but he also devoted his time and energies to raising additional funds in the United States of America.

8. Passing a scruffy looking woman in obvious need in the streets outside of the Vatican, an empathetic knight stopped a few steps past her. Returning he gave her what little change he had. She accepted, saying "he" sometimes comes out at night when all others have gone away, dressed in ordinary clothes, attended by a guard, and gives money to us just as you do. She pointed up to the Holy Father's apartment.

The transcendent foundation of Largesse lies in the First Beatitude, which states, "Blessed are the poor in spirit." The beatitudes start with the word "blessed." This indicates that those who follow such counsel will be made happy by God. This happiness is of a supernatural quality and becomes a source of fuel for the soul, energizing the spirit.

"Poor in spirit" means not to be enslaved by anything in this world. It means to be internally free and spiritually separated, that is, detached from everything except God. Whatever one possesses— material wealth, intellectual ability, social prestige—before God, one is to be detached as a condition for authentic happiness here, and later in heaven. Thus the reward of the Fourth Beatitude is attained, "For they shall have the kingdom of heaven."

The foundation of Largesse is the state of being "poor in spirit" through which one has a foretaste of the sublime happiness awaiting in heaven. Happiness is conditioned upon the detachment from everything in this world. Our Holy Father tells us to look for Christ in those at the margins of society and champion them. Our hearts are to be set on God. In the final analysis, "the measure in which our hearts are set on Him, in that measure we shall experience heavenly joy here."

Further quoting a holy knight, St. Sir Ignatius of Loyola:

"Dear Lord, teach me to be generous, teach me to serve you as you deserve, to give and not to count the cost, to fight and not to heed the wound, to toil and not to seek for rest, to labor and not to seek reward, save that of knowing that I do your will."

# IV

# The Order in the United States: American Lieutenancies

*My mind, Time's enemy, Oblivion's foe,*
*Disposer true of each noteworthy thing,*
*Oh, let thy virtuous might avail me so,*
*That I each troop and captain great may sing,*
*That in this glorious war did famous grow,*
*Forgot till now by Time's evil handling:*
*This work, derived from my treasures dear,*
*Let all times hearken, never age outwear.*

*Jerusalem Delivered* by Torquato Tasso (1544–1595)
translated by Edward Fairfax (1560–1635)
First Book, Stanza XXXVI

# CHAPTER 27

# THE ORDER OF THE HOLY SEPULCHRE OF JERUSALEM IN THE UNITED STATES OF AMERICA

The dictum of the Holy Father in 1907 authorized a new constitution for the Order. It provided for the organization of National Lieutenancies, which brought about a rapid expansion of the Order. However, it wasn't until 1926 that the first American Lieutenancy was organized by the Reverend Monsignor Abraham D'Assemani as the representative of the then Latin Patriarch of Jerusalem, His Beatitude Louis Barlassina. The Lieutenancy was formally established on April 30, 1929 with Monsignor D'Assemani and other dignitaries who administered the Order. The Constitution and Bylaws of the Order for the American Lieutenancy were adopted with the approval of the Latin Patriarch, who was the Rector and Perpetual Administrator of the Order at that time. The first Grand Prior was His Eminence Denis Cardinal Dougherty, Archbishop of Philadelphia, Pennsylvania. Monsignor D'Assemani was succeeded by Chief Justice Victor Dowling of New York. The third Lieutenant was Sir Michael Francis Doyle of Philadelphia.

Records are not available to determine the persons who were Knights and Ladies prior to the establishment of the first American Lieutenancy. Unfortunately, no information is available in the interval between April 1929 to June 1940, when the American Lieutenancy was divided into the Eastern and Western Lieutenancies. Immediately following the division, a brilliant reception and banquet was held at the Waldorf Astoria Hotel in New York City. Thirty-six persons were in attendance. Addresses were delivered by His Eminence Denis Cardinal Dougherty, Grand Prior of the Eastern Lieutenancy; His Eminence Francis J. Cardinal Spellman, Archbishop of New York; His Excellency, Most Reverend Francis J. Kelley, Bishop of Oklahoma City and Tulsa, newly appointed Grand Prior of the Western Lieutenancy; Chief Justice Joseph Taryan of New York; and His Excellency, Sir Michael Francis Doyle, KGCHS, Lieutenant of the Eastern Lieutenancy. Bishop Kelley initially served as both Lieutenant and Grand Prior of the new Western Lieutenancy. The emphasis of all addresses was the purpose of the Order, pointing out that due to the devastation of war throughout Europe, the responsibility of the preservation of the Faith in the Holy Land must fall upon the American Knights and Ladies.

Included in the Order at the time of the division of the American Lieutenancy were the following prelates:

**Their Eminences:**
H.E. William Cardinal O'Connell, KGCHS
    Archbishop of Boston
H.E. Denis Cardinal Dougherty, KGCHS
    Archbishop of Philadelphia
H.E. Patrick Cardinal Hayes, KGCHS
    Archbishop of New York
H.E. Francis Cardinal Spellman, KGCHS
    Archbishop of New York (then in Boston)
H.E. Samuel Cardinal Stritch, KGCHS
    Archbishop of Chicago (then in Tulsa)

**Their Excellencies, Most Reverend:**
H.E. John J. Cantwell, KGCHS
    Archbishop of Los Angeles
H.E. Michael F. Gallagher, KGCHS
    Bishop of Detroit
H.E. Urban J. Vehr, KCHS
    Archbishop of Denver
H.E. Francis J. Kelley, KGCHS
    Bishop of Oklahoma City and Tulsa
H.E. Frank A. Thill, KCHS
    Bishop of Concordia (now Salina)
H.E. Christian H. Winkleman, KCHS
    Bishop of Wichita
H.E. Christopher E. Byrne, KCHS
    Bishop of Galveston
H.E. Gerald F. O'Hara, KCHS
    Bishop of Savannah and Atlanta
H.E. Edwin V. O'Hara, KCHS
    Bishop of Kansas City

**Among the laity were the following:**
John J. Craig, KGCHS, Tulsa
Joe Zach Miller III, KGCHS, Kansas City
Edward A. Doheny, KGCHS, Los Angeles
Ignatius J. O'Shaughnessy, KGCHS, St. Paul
Francis J. Hogan, KGCHS, Los Angeles
William J. Sherry, KGCHS, Tulsa
William J. Connelly, KGCHS, Tulsa
William F. Warren, KGCHS, Tulsa

Records at the Vatican show eighty-five Knights and Ladies registered with the Secretary of State to the Holy See on November 26, 1946 as follows:

| | | | |
|---|---|---|---|
| Argyl | 1 | New York | 14 |
| Birmingham | 1 | Omaha | 1 |
| Brooklyn | 2 | Owensboro | 1 |
| Charleston | 1 | Pasadena | 1 |
| Chicago | 1 | Philadelphia | 2 |
| Denver | 1 | Rochester | 1 |
| Detroit | 1 | St. Louis | 2 |
| Galveston | 7 | St. Paul | 3 |
| Kansas City | 4 | Salford | 1 |
| Leavenworth | 1 | Santa Fe | 1 |
| Los Angeles | 6 | Savannah | 1 |
| Louisville | 1 | Southmark | 1 |
| Lowell | 1 | Springfield, MA | 4 |
| Milwaukee | 1 | Tulsa | 19 |
| New Orleans | 1 | Union City | 1 |
| | | Wichita | 2 |

Thereafter the growth of the Order in the United States was rapid, spearheaded by the author as Vice Governor General, but particularly his successor, Sir F. Russell Kendall, Knight of the Collar, both of the United States. The Order in the United States at the end of 1997 is organized in nine Lieutenancies, and approximates nine thousand Knights and Ladies, slightly less than one-half of the world's total, which is 19,000.

Others that should be given credit for the rapid expansion of the Order in the United States include:

**Their Excellencies:**
Sir John J. Craig, KGCHS
       Knight of the Collar of Merit
       Former Western and Southern Lieutenancy
Sir William J. Doyle, KGCHS
       First Lieutenant of the present Western Lieutenancy
Sir Frank M. Folsom, KGCHS
       Eastern Lieutenancy

The Lieutenancies of the United States and the dates of their formation:

1940    The American Lieutenancy was divided into the Eastern and Western Lieutenancies.

1963    The Western Lieutenancy was divided into the Southern and Northern Lieutenancies.

1965    The Northern Delegation was formed and in 1967 it became the Northern Lieutenancy.

1973    The Western States of the Southern Lieutenancy formed a new Western Lieutenancy.

1981    The New England States, except for Connecticut, were taken from the Eastern Lieutenancy to form a Northeastern Lieutenancy.

1982    Puerto Rico Province was taken from the Southern Lieutenancy to form a Magistral Delegation, and in 1996 became the Lieutenancy of Puerto Rico.

1986    The Northern Lieutenancy was divided into the Northern and North Central Lieutenancies.

1986    The Southern Lieutenancy was divided into the Southeastern and Southwestern Lieutenancies with Washington D.C. and certain States of the Eastern Lieutenancies added to the new Southeastern Lieutenancy.

1993    Delaware, Maryland, Washington D.C., Virginia, West Virginia, Tennessee, and North Carolina were taken from the Eastern and Southeastern Lieutenancies to form the Middle Atlantic Lieutenancy.

1993    Oregon, Washington, Idaho, Montana, Wyoming, Alaska, and that part of California north of but not including Santa Barbara were taken from the Western Lieutenancy to form the Northwestern Lieutenancy.

At the end of 1997 the total Confreres and Consoeurs of the Equestrian Order of the Holy Sepulchre of Jerusalem in the United States of America was approximately nine thousand.

# CHAPTER 28

# EASTERN LIEUTENANCY: 1940 TO THE PRESENT

The Eastern Lieutenancy is currently composed of the four eastern states of New Jersey, Pennsylvania, New York, and Connecticut. Over the years, the following Knights served as Lieutenants, Their Excellencies:

| | |
|---|---|
| Sir Michael Francis Doyle, KGCHS | 1938–1945 |
| Sir Raoul E. Desvernine, KGCHS | 1946–1950 |
| Sir Frank M. Folsom, KGCHS | 1951–1960 |
| Sir Victor D. Ziminsky, KGCHS | 1961–1977 |
| Sir John M. Joyce, KGCHS | 1978–1983 |
| Sir Joseph G. Kearns, KGCHS | 1984–1985 |
| Sir Thomas M. Macioce, KGCHS | 1986–1990 |
| Sir George Doty, KGCHS | 1991–1992 |
| Sir Martin J. Moran, KGCHS | 1993–Present |

The Grand Priors during these years inclued Their Eminences:

| | |
|---|---|
| Denis Cardinal Dougherty, KGCHS | 1940–1945 |
| Richard Cardinal Cushing, KGCHS | 1946–1950 |
| Francis Cardinal Spellman, KGCHS | 1951–1967 |
| Terence Cardinal Cooke, KGCHS | 1968–1983 |
| John Cardinal O'Connor, KGCHS | 1984–Present |

At the end of 1990, the Eastern Lieutenancy had a total of Confreres and Consoeurs of 1,437 of which 1,391 were lay persons. The 46 clergy included 18 Bishops and 1 Cardinal.

## Sir George Doty, KGCHS

For a number of years, on entering the Rotunda of the Holy Sepulchre, the pilgrim was struck with the sharp contrast between the illumination of the Spirit at the site of the risen Christ and the darkness that hovered over it in the shape of tubular scaffolding, which signified the folly of mankind by the divisions of our common faith. Restorations of the Basilica of the Holy Sepulchre in Jerusalem had begun in

*H.E. Sir George E. Doty, KGCHS*

1967 and had progressed by the early 1990s to where most of the makeshift shoring and supporting scaffolding had been removed revealing a stronger and more beautiful edifice. However, agreement could not be reached among the religious groups—the Franciscans, the Greek Orthodox, and Armenian Churches on the redecoration of the dome above the rotunda, and restoration had been delayed for technical, financial, and legal difficulties.

Into the gloom came Sir George Doty, Knight Grand Cross of the Holy Sepulchre, Lieutenant of the Eastern Lieutenancy of the Equestrian Order of the Holy Sepulchre of Jerusalem from 1991 to 1992, whom Christ motivated with holy graces and raised up as His champion. True to the chivalric virtues of Charité and Largesse, Sir George took it upon himself to resolve the problem. With a self-reliance that speaks to the core of Charité, he inquired as to the reason behind this shame. He faced the status quo that had been set by bribery in the eighteenth century and sealed in the nineteenth century as a result of Crimean and Russo-Turkish warfare.[3] Sir George determined to break through the dispute and restore the dome. He contacted Fr. Denis Madden of the Pontifical Mission for Palestine.

Sir George armed Fr. Denis with the assurance that he would provide whatever resources necessary to restore the dome. Thus fortified, Fr. Denis conducted discreet negotiations between the involved parties: the Custodian of the Holy Land, Fr. Giuseppe Nazzaro, O.F.M., the Greek Orthodox Patriarch, Diodoros I, and the Armenian Patriarch, Torkom Manougian. Fr. Denis succeeded in assuring the three parties that Sir George had no intention of altering the status quo, but had every intention of honoring Our Lord, Jesus Christ and glorifying the Holy Sepulchre. The parties assessed that Sir George was truly generous to the Lord and voted to accept his unselfish offer.

Sir George had been impressed by a Fresno, California artist, Ara Normart, and

---

3."The Basilica of the Holy Sepulchre in Jerusalem", G.S.P. Freeman-Grenville, Carta, Jerusalem, 1994, p34–40 recommended him to Fr. Denis. After presenting his sketches to the Patriarchs and the Custodian, they debated and ultimately settled on a design. A skylight is located in the center of the soaring dome letting in natural sunlight. "Twelve golden rays on a pearl-colored background... accentuate the natural brightness streaming in from the lantern (its panes have all been replaced and from the artificial light released by powerful lamps concealed behind the rays). These are intended to symbolize the twelve Apostles and the Church's expansion in the world. Each ray is tripartite to symbolize the mystery of the Triune God."[4] Additionally, gold stars accentuate the "explosion of light" at Jesus' resurrection.[5]

"The significance is not the artwork," said Ara Normart. "It's the fact that the three churches got together and agreed after so many years."

*His Eminence John Cardinal O'Connor, KGCHS, Grand Prior and H.E. Sir Martin J. Moran, KGCHS, Lieutenant*

The new dome was unveiled to the ring of Church bells and applause in an ecumenical celebration that brought together the leaders of the Christian Churches in the Holy Land as well as many secular dignitaries including the Mayor of Jerusalem, Mr. Ehud Olmert, senior officials of the Ministry for Religious Affairs for the Israeli Government, the Palestinian Authority's ministers Hassan Tabboob for worship and Faisal el Hussenini for Jerusalem, accompanied by Chairman Arafat's chief of staff, Mr. Ramzi Khoury, and Messrs. Hashrawi and Jarjouri, Christian deputies of the Jerusalem jurisdiction to the Authority's Council. The consuls general of European Christian nations, including Greece, as well as the Apostolic Delegate for Jerusalem and Palestine and the Apostolic Nuncio in Israel, Archbishop Andrea Cordero Lanza di Montezemolo attended. Msgr. Robert Stern, President of the Pontifical Mission for Palestine accompanied Fr. Denis Madden, Ara Normart, Sir George Doty, KGCHS, and his wife Marie Doty, LGCHS.

---

4. "Jerusalem's Basilica Dome is Restored," Graziano Motta, L'Osservatore Romano, N.8-19 February 1997

5. "Holy Sepulcher Face Lift Unveiled in Jerusalem," Hilary Appelman, The Washington Times, 3 January 1997, pA12

"This is a day of great joy for us," said Sir George. "We're all children of God, hoping for the same future. It is gratifying to see how much can be accomplished when men of good will go forward courageously together."

*Dome of the Rotunda, Church of the Holy Sepulchre*

# CHAPTER 29

# SOUTHERN LIEUTENANCY: 1963 TO 1986

The Southern Lieutenancy of the United States came into existence in 1963, at a time when the United States was made up of just two Lieutenancies—the Eastern and the Western, with the Mississippi River as the dividing line. The domestic growth of the Order west of the Mississippi led the Grand Magisterium of the Order in Rome to make a further division of what was then the Western Lieutenancy. The name "Western Lieutenancy" was dropped, and the territory west of the Mississippi River was divided into a new Southern Lieutenancy and a Northern Delegation. At the time of the division, the old Western Lieutenancy consisted of 242 Confreres and Consoeurs.

John J. Craig, KGCHS, of Tulsa, Oklahoma became the Lieutenant of the new Southern Lieutenancy with the Most Rev. Thomas K. Gorman, Bishop of Dallas-Fort Worth as the Grand Prior. The territory of the new Southern Lieutenancy was made up of the States of Tennessee, Alabama, Mississippi, Louisiana, Arkansas, Oklahoma, Kansas, Texas, New Mexico, Arizona, Colorado, Nevada, California, Oregon, Washington, Alaska, and the Hawaiian Islands.

The Northern Delegation comprised the remaining States of the old Western Lieutenancy with Joe Zach Miller III of Kansas City, Missouri, being named the Delegate. The Most Rev. Leo Binz, Archbishop of St. Paul was appointed as the Northern Delegation's new Grand Prior. At that time, the Northern Delegation had a total Confreres and Consoeurs of 71 Knights and 21 Ladies.

The first annual meeting of the Southern Lieutenancy took place in Fort Worth, Texas in the fall of 1963. In 1964 the annual meeting and investiture was held in Wichita, Kansas. In 1965 the Northern Delegation was the host for a meeting and investiture in St. Paul, Minnesota. In 1966 the Knights and Ladies gathered in Austin, Texas, for their annual meeting. On February 16, 1967, the Northern Delegation officially became the Northern Lieutenancy and thus became independent of the Southern Lieutenancy.

On March 19 of the same year, in recognition of the rapid growth of the Order in the western states, the Grand Magisterium formed a Western Delegation with Roger Freeman, KGCHS, of California being named the Western Delegate. The Most Rev. Leo T. Maher, Bishop of San Diego, was appointed to the position of Grand Prior for the new Western Delegation.

The 1968 meeting of the Southern Lieutenancy occurred in Santa Fe, New Mexico, while in 1969 and 1970 the Knights and Ladies gathered in Houston and New Orleans. Also in 1970, an investiture was held for the Western Delegation in San Diego, at which time more than 50 Knights and Ladies were invested. In 1971 the annual meeting took place in Fort Worth, in 1972 at San Diego, and in 1973 at Denver.

With the continued growth of the Order on the West Coast, the Grand Magisterium announced on June 29, 1973 that the Western Delegation had been elevated to a full-fledged Lieutenancy with Dr. William J. Doyle, KGCHS, of LaJolla, California as the Lieutenant. Bishop Maher continued as Grand Prior. With the creation of the Western Lieutenancy, the Southern Lieutenancy lost Colorado, Kansas, and all of the states west of New Mexico including Alaska and Hawaii.

On October 27, 1973, Sir F. Russell Kendall, later Knight of the Collar, of Houston was appointed by the Grand Magisterium as the Lieutenant of the Southern Lieutenancy, succeeding Sir John J. Craig, KGCHS. The Most Rev. John J. Cassata, Bishop of Fort Worth, was appointed to the post of Grand Prior.

At the time of the appointments of Bishop Cassata and Kendall, the Grand Magisterium also rearranged the Lieutenancies of the United States. After the realignment, the Southern Lieutenancy was made up of the States of New Mexico, Oklahoma, Texas, Arkansas, Louisiana, Mississippi, Tennessee, Alabama, Georgia, North and South Carolina, Florida, Puerto Rico, and the Virgin Islands. After the creation of the Western Lieutenancy, the Southern Lieutenancy had a total Confreres and Consoeurs of 450 Knights and Ladies.

During the 1983 meeting in Tulsa it was announced that the Grand Magisterium had appointed Lieutenant Kendall to the position of Vice Governor General of the Order, succeeding Alfred J. Blasco, Knight of the Collar, of Kansas City, who had announced his retirement. Sir Kendall was succeeded by Sir Clayton J. Charbonnet, KGCHS, of New Orleans as Lieutenant. At the same time, Bishop Casatta announced his retirement as Grand Prior. The Grand Magisterium appointed the Most Rev. Stanley T. Ott, Bishop of Baton Rouge, as the new Grand Prior.

In 1984, the first year under Charbonnet's leadership, the Lieutenancy held its meeting and investiture in Dallas, Texas, at which time a total of 143 new Knights and Ladies were invested. After the 1984 investiture, the Confreres and Consoeurs of the Southern Lieutenancy totaled 455 Knights, 495 Ladies, and 120 Clergy Knights, a total of 1,070 according to an announcement by Sir Clayton Charbonnet.[6] With the rapid growth of the Southern Lieutenancy, the Grand Magisterium of the Order in 1986 divided this Lieutenancy into the Southeastern and Southwestern Lieutenancies with Washington, D.C. and certain states of the Eastern Lieutenancy added to the Southeastern Lieutenancy. The Most Reverend Stanley Ott, Bishop of Baton Rouge, remained as Grand Prior.

---

6. Deceased 1996

# CHAPTER 30

# SOUTHEASTERN LIEUTENANCY: 1986 TO THE PRESENT

The Southeastern Lieutenancy of the Order of the Holy Sepulchre of Jerusalem came into being in 1986 when it was decreed by the Grand Magisterium in Rome that the Southern Lieutenancy was to be divided into two separate lieutenancies. At the final banquet of the Southern Lieutenancy held in Corpus Christi, Texas, Sir F. Russell Kendall, Knight of the Collar, Vice Governor General of the Order, announced that the new Southeastern Lieutenancy was to be made up of the States of Louisiana, Alabama, Florida, Georgia, Mississippi, North and South Carolina, Tennessee, Virginia, West Virginia, the Archdiocese of Washington, D.C., and the Diocese of the Virgin Islands, which is suffragan to Washington.

Sir Clayton J. Charbonnet, KGCHS, of New Orleans, who had been Lieutenant of the Southern Lieutenancy, was named Lieutenant of the new Southeastern Lieutenancy. The Most Rev. Stanley J. Ott, Bishop of Baton Rouge, Louisiana, who had been Grand Prior of the Southern Lieutenancy, was appointed to fill the same post for the Southeastern Lieutenancy. The new lieutenancy started its existence with a total of 694 Confreres and Consoeurs domiciled in 10 states, plus the Archdiocese of Washington, D.C.

Sir F. Russell Kendall pointed out that the Lieutenancy occupied a unique place in the Order, when he said: "With ten states and part of an eleventh state, together with our nation's capital, you have a vast territory, most of which has been traditionally known throughout the world as 'The Deep South'. This area offers great potential and a serious challenge to each of you." The area of the new lieutenancy includes sections of the nation in which the Protestant tradition is strong, and where Catholics are few. Catholics are most numerous in Louisiana and Florida, each of which contains seven Dioceses. Each of the other states, except South Carolina have only two Dioceses, while South Carolina has only one.

The Southeastern Lieutenancy held its first meeting and investiture on September 26–27, 1987, in Pensacola, Florida. There were almost 600 Knights and Ladies attending, including 110 investees. Among the dignitaries present were the Most Reverend Archbishop Pio Laghi,[7] the Apostolic Pro-Nuncio in the United

---

7. Now Cardinal residing in Rome

*H.E. Sir George H. Toye, KGCHS*
(Photo by Mike Posey)

States and himself a Knight of the Lieutenancy, the Vice Governor General, Sir F. Russell Kendall of Houston, Texas, and 18 bishops. Three of the Bishops were invested into the Order: the Most Rev. John C. Favalora,[8] Bishop of Alexandria, Louisiana, the Most Rev. Sean O'Malley,[9] OFMC, former Bishop of St. Thomas in the Virgin Islands, and the Most Rev. Harry Flynn, at that time Bishop Coadjutor of Lafayette, Louisiana.

The weekend program began with a Memorial Mass dedicated to the five Knights and Ladies who died during the previous year, including the Most Rev. Joseph G. Vath, Bishop of Birmingham, Alabama. The Most Reverend James Cardinal Hickey, Archbishop of Washington, D.C., was the homilist at the Memorial Mass. He pointed out that Knights and Ladies should be proud of the Order's ancient past, but that a new Crusade was needed in the present to insure that all who live in the Holy Land do so with peace and dignity.

Archbishop Laghi was the speaker at the first annual banquet of the Lieutenancy, and called upon all Knights and Ladies to redouble their efforts in support of Catholicism in the Near East and asked them to work for peace in the region. Sir Bernard J. Ficarra, KGCHS, was awarded the Silver Palm of Jerusalem. At the end of the program, Lieutenant Charbonnet announced that the total Confreres and Consoeurs in the Lieutenancy, including the 1987 investees, were at 363 Lay Knights, 364 Ladies and 77 Clergy Knights, for a total of 804. At the end of 1989, the Lieutenancy had a total of 837 lay people and 212 clergy, of which 30 were bishops.

At the end of the 1990 Annual Meeting of the Southeastern Lieutenancy, held in Washington, D.C., Sir Clayton Charbonnet announced his retirement. The Cardinal Grand Master, His Eminence Joseph Cardinal Caprio, announced the appointment of Sir George H. Toye, KGCHS, as the new Lieutenant. Investees at the Investiture numbered 97 lay persons and 28 clergy including 7 bishops. Total Confreres and

---

8. At present, the Archbishop of Miami
9. The current Bishop of Fall River, Mass.

Consoeurs numbered 1,090 of which 933 were lay persons and 157 were clergy including 39 bishops. This surge in numbers was a great tribute to the leadership of Sir Clayton Charbonnet.

The first meeting of the Southeastern Lieutenancy under Lieutenant George H. Toye was held in Louisiana on October 26 and 27 of 1991. The Host Bishop was H.E. Most Reverend Harry Flynn, KC*HS, Bishop of Lafayette. The general chairpersons were Sir J. Dan Bouligny, Section Representative for the Diocese of Lafayette and his wife, Lady Jacqueline Bouligny. The Lieutenancy was privileged to invest H.E. Most Reverend Edward A. McCarthy, Archbishop of Miami, Florida, along with fourteen priests, one deacon and one hundred and fifteen Knights and Ladies. H.E. Clayton Charbonnet was named Lieutenant of Honor by the Grand Master, His Eminence Joseph Cardinal Caprio. Upon the request of the Lieutenant, H.E. George H. Toye, the Grand Master conferred the Gold Palm of Jerusalem upon the Grand Prior of the Lieutenancy, Most Reverend Stanley J. Ott, KC*HS, and upon H.E. Clayton Charbonnet, KGCHS, in recognition for outstanding service to the Order and to the Church in the Holy Land. The Lieutenant read the letter of appointment while outlining the services and accomplishments of the honorees. Celebrating the first meeting of the Lieutenancy under Lieutenant Toye was the late Most Reverend Peter Canisius van Lierde of Rome, Vicar General Emeritus to Pope John Paul II, and 18 other archbishops and bishops. The strength of the Lieutenancy stood at 1201 Knights and Ladies. The principle speaker at the Sunday evening banquet was the Most Reverend Stanley J. Ott, KC*HS, Grand Prior.

In November of 1991, the Most Reverend Michel Sabbah, Latin Patriarch of Jerusalem, visited New Orleans and was received at a Mass, reception, and dinner by the Knights and Ladies of the New Orleans Diocese. The plea of the Patriarch was for Justice and Peace in the Middle East.

The second meeting of the Southeastern Lieutenancy was held in Naples (Diocese of Venice), Florida, on September 12 and 13, 1992, and had as the Host Bishop, H.E. Most Reverend John Nevins, KC*HS. Sir William E. Ball and Lady Alma Ball were General Chairpersons of the weekend. The annual souvenir booklet received by all of the Knights and Ladies featured a brilliant picture of a painting of Sir Godfrey de Bouillon, Advocatus Sancti Sepulchri, painted by Jeronimo de Espinosa (1600-1680) of the Spanish School and containing the following writing relative to Sir Godfrey:

> In the year 1095 Pope Urban II proclaimed the First Crusade for the Liberation of the Holy Land from the Mohammedans, and with the rally cry of Deus Lo Vult! God wills it!

### The Crimson Cross shall be to you the assurance of victory or the palm of martyrdom

> Godfrey, Duke of Lorraine, a direct descendant of Charlemagne, was at that time about thirty-five years of age. Well-schooled, he could read

and write and speak Latin and the Romance languages as well as German. A captain in the army in his teens, he had carried a standard in the service of his liege lord, Henry IV of Germany. His personal courage was beyond question. Nobility of character was his likewise: and purity of life. A contemporary has described him this way: "He was handsome, tall, agreeable, moral, and at the same time so gentle in his manner that he seemed better fitted to be a monk than a knight. But when enemies appeared before him and combat was at hand, his soul was filled with the caring of a lion, and he had no fears for himself. What shield, what buckler could withstand the fall of his sword."

But how to equip the First Crusade?

Godfrey was wealthy. Lord of gray-walled Bouillon, Marquis of Antwerp, Duke of Lorraine, he was master of wide forests and broad lands. His were the richest fiefs of the Rhineland. He sold the City of Metz for one hundred thousand crowns, disposed of two principalities, and even pawned Bouillon.

The Crusade began on about August 14, 1096. Jerusalem was taken on Friday afternoon, July 15, 1099. The Cross was above the Crescent; the Holy City and the Sepulchre of Our Lord were in Christian hands. One week after the capture of Jerusalem the Crusaders met in council and chose Godfrey the King of Jerusalem. Remembering a crown of thorns, he humbly refused to accept the honor. However, he took the title of Defender of the Holy Sepulchre. Godfrey of Bouillon, soldier of soldiers, warrior of warriors, and Catholic Knight, died July 18, 1100 and was buried at the foot of Calvary.

The Lieutenancy was privileged to invest Most Reverend Raymond Lessard, Bishop of the Diocese of Savannah, Georgia, and Most Reverend James Lyke, Archbishop of Atlanta, 17 priests and 75 Knights and Ladies. The Sunday evening banquet had as the principle speaker, the Most Reverend Oscar Lipscomb, Archbishop of Mobile. It was announced that weekend that the Lieutenancy would sponsor a pilgrimage to Jerusalem led by the Lieutenant, H.E. George Toye and under the guide of Reverend Godfrey Kloetzle of the Terra Sancta College of Jerusalem. The pilgrims would also spend four days in Rome and would attend the audience of Pope John Paul II. Also announced was the strength of the Lieutenancy which then stood at 1292 Knights and Ladies.

On April 27, 1992, H.E. George H. Toye, Lieutenant of the Southeastern Lieutenancy, made a request of the Grand Magisterium of the Order through a letter to H.E. Count Ludovico Carducci Artenisio, that the Grand Cross of Merit with Gold Star be presented to The Honorable James A. Baker, III, Secretary of State of the United States of America in recognition of the vast efforts he made for the cause of peace throughout the world, and more particular, in the area of the Middle East that is known as the "Holy Land" and the Apostolate of the Equestrian Order of the Holy Sepulchre of Jerusalem.

Catholics and non-Catholics of distinction may be awarded the various degrees of Merit of the Equestrian Order of the Holy Sepulchre of Jerusalem, the highest of which is The Grand Cross of Merit with Gold Star. This mark of distinction is very seldom conferred and then only to personages of the greatest merit. At the time of the Presentation, The Honorable James A. Baker, III, was Chief of Staff and Senior Counselor to the President of the United States of America.

The request was granted and the presentation was made on September 23 by the Cardinal Grand Master of the Order, His Eminence Guiseppe Cardinal Caprio at a reception at the Vatican Embassy in Washington, D.C. Present at the reception were His Eminence Guiseppe Cardinal Caprio, Most Reverend Agostino Cacciavillan, KC*HS, Apostolic Pro-Nuncio; H.E. Count Ludovico Carducci Artenisio, the Governor General of the Order, and Countess Rheine Artenisio; H.E. F. Russell Kendall, Vice Governor General of the Order and Lady Anne Kendall; H.E. Norman MacNeil, Lieutenant of the Northeastern Lieutenancy and Lady Phyllis MacNeil; H.E. Andrew J. Layden, Lieutenant of the Southwestern Lieutenancy and Lady Alberta Layden; H.E. Matthew Lamb, Lieutenant of the North Central Lieutenancy and Lady Rose Lamb; H.E. George H. Toye, Lieutenant of the Southeastern Lieutenancy and Lady Leontine Toye; Mrs. Susan Baker, their children and staff.

The Lieutenancy suffered a serious loss that year with the death of the Grand Prior, H.E. Most Reverend Stanley J. Ott, KC*HS, Bishop of Baton Rouge, Louisiana, on Saturday, November 28. Bishop Ott was appointed Grand Prior of the Southern Lieutenancy in 1984 when Bishop John Cassata of Fort Worth announced his retirement. When the Southern Lieutenancy was split into the Southeastern and Southwestern Lieutenancies in 1986, Bishop Ott remained the Grand Prior of the Southeastern Lieutenancy. One of his first official acts was to preside at the Annual Meeting and Investiture in Lafayette, Louisiana. At the request of the Lieutenant, the Grand Magisterium appointed H.E. Most Reverend Francis Bible Schulte, Archbishop of New Orleans, as the new Grand Prior.

At this time in its history, the Southeastern Lieutenancy was privileged to have in its hierarchy, His Eminence James Cardinal Hickey, KGCHS, Archbishop of Washington; Most Reverend Agostino Cacciavillan, KC*HS, Apostolic Pro-Nuncio to the United States of America; along with 7Archbishops and 33 Bishops.

The third meeting of the Lieutenancy, held in New Orleans on September 18 and 19, 1993, was preceded by a mini-consulta and attended by H.E. Count Ludovico Carducci Artenisio, the Governor General of the Order and Knight of the Collar; H.E. F. Russell Kendall, Vice Governor General and Knight of the Collar; H.E. Alfred J. Blasco, Member of the Grand Magisterium and Knight of Collar; H.E. George H. Toye, KGCHS, Lieutenant of the Southeastern Lieutenancy; H.E. Anthony Adducci, KGCHS, Lieutenant of the Northern Lieutenancy; H.E. Andrew J. Layden, KGCHS, Lieutenant of the Southwestern Lieutenancy; H.E. Martin J.

Moran, KGCHS, Lieutenant of the Eastern Lieutenancy; H.E. Matthew E. Lamb, KGCHS, Lieutenant of the North Central Lieutenancy; H.E. George Zorn, KGCHS, Lieutenant of the Western Lieutenancy; H.E. Norman E. MacNeil, KGCHS, Lieutenant of the Northeastern Lieutenancy; H.E. Luis Sala, KGCHS, Lieutenant of Puerto Rico; H.E. Ricardo Triana Uribe, KGCHS, Lieutenant of Bogota, Columbia; H.E. William B Guyol, KGCHS, Lieutenant Elect of the Northern Lieutenancy; H.E. Bernard J. Ficarra, KGCHS, Lieutenant Elect of the Middle Atlantic Lieutenancy; and H.E. Clayton Charbonnet, KGCHS, Lieutenant of Honor of the Southeastern Lieutenancy. This third meeting had as the Host Bishop the new Grand Prior of the Lieutenancy, H.E. Most Reverend Francis B. Schulte, Archbishop of New Orleans.

The Investiture was held in the Basilica-Cathedral of St. Louis, King of France. The Lieutenancy was privileged to invest H.E. Most Reverend Michael Jarrell, Bishop of Houma-Thibodaux; H.E. Most Reverend Edward O. Kmiec, Bishop of Nashville, Tennessee; H.E. Most Reverend Robert W. Muench, Auxiliary Bishop of New Orleans; H.E. Most Reverend Dominic Carmon, Auxiliary Bishop of New Orleans; 20 priests and 70 Knights and Ladies. The strength of the Lieutenancy was then numbered at 1363. The Gold Palm of Jerusalem was presented to our Ecclesiastical Master of Ceremonies, Reverend Monsignor Elmo Romagosa, KCHS, for his many years of service to the Order and devotion to our Apostolate.

At the white-tie banquet that Sunday evening our guest speakers were the Governor General, H.E. Count Ludovico Carducci Artenisio and H.E. F. Russell Kendall. The latter announced the formation of the Middle Atlantic Lieutenancy appointing H.E. Bernard J. Ficarra as the Lieutenant. Washington D.C., Virginia, West Virginia, Tennessee, and North Carolina were taken from the Southeastern Lieutenancy to form part of the Middle Atlantic Lieutenancy. There followed a presentation of the flags of the States that were transferred to the newly formed Lieutenancy from the Southeastern Lieutenancy. Remaining in the Southeastern Lieutenancy are the states of Louisiana, Mississippi, Alabama, Florida, Georgia, and South Carolina.

On May 17, 1994 the Lieutenant of the Southeastern Lieutenancy, H.E. George H. Toye, attended the 1994 Consulta of the Order at its Vatican Headquarters in Rome, Italy. This was a five-day meeting and attended by the Lieutenants of the Order throughout the World numbering 44.

The fourth meeting of the Southeastern Lieutenancy was held on October 15 and 16, 1994 in the Archdiocese of Atlanta, Georgia. Our Host Bishop was H.E. Most Reverend John F. Donoghue, Archbishop of Atlanta. The Diocesan Coordinator was Reverend Monsignor Edward J. Dillon, KHS, and the general chairpersons were Sir Crofton A. Breuer, KCHS, and Lady Hermione K. Breuer, LCHS. The Lieutenancy was privileged to invest Most Reverend David E. Foley, Bishop of Birmingham; Most Reverend John J. Snyder, Bishop of St. Augustine, 10 priests and 74 Knights and Ladies. The strength of the Lieutenancy was 1171 at this time. The guest speaker for the weekend was Reverend David Marie Jaeger, OMI.

The fifth meeting of the Southeastern Lieutenancy was held in the Archdiocese of Miami, Florida, on September 16 and 17, 1995. The Host Bishop was Most Reverend John C. Favalora, Archbishop of Miami. The general chairpersons were Sir Jorge J. Bosch, KC*HS, and Lady Yvelise Bosch, LC*HS. Our guest speaker for the banquet on Sunday evening was Reverend Father Peter Vasko, O.F.M., the English Definitor of the Custody of the Holy Land. Eleven priests and 86 Knights and Ladies were invested.

The sixth meeting of the Lieutenancy was held in the Diocese of St. Petersburg on September 21 and 22, 1996. The Host Bishop was Most Reverend Robert N. Lynch, Bishop of St. Petersburg. The general chairpersons were Sir Douglas Conner, KC*HS, and Lady Elizabeth Conner, LC*HS. Twenty-six Knights and Ladies were awarded the Silver Palm of Jerusalem for their faithful participation in the Apostolate of the Equestrian Order of the Holy Sepulchre of Jerusalem for more than twenty-five years. The Gold Palm of Jerusalem was presented to Reverend Father James Russo for his efforts to the Lieutenancy as Ecclesiastical Master of Ceremonies for many years. The Lieutenancy was privileged to invest the Host Bishop, Most Rev. Robert N. Lynch, 13 priests, 1 Deacon and 66 Knights and Ladies. The guest speaker for the Sunday evening formal banquet was the Most Rev. Thomas G. Doran, Bishop of Rockford, Illinois, and a member of the Grand Magisterium of our Order.

The Lieutenancy sponsored two pilgrimages: the first on November 7 through 21, 1993 and the second November 8 through 22, 1996, both led by the Lieutenant and included visits to the Holy Land and Rome.

*H.E. Most Rev. Francis B. Schulte,*
*KGCHS*

# CHAPTER 31

# MIDDLE ATLANTIC LIEUTENANCY: 1993 TO THE PRESENT

The Middle Atlantic Lieutenancy of the Equestrian Order of the Holy Sepulchre of Jerusalem came into being on 15 September 1993 with the following proclamation by His Excellency, Count Ludovico Carducci Artenisio, Governor General, Knight of the Collar, as promulgated by the Cardinal Grand Master in Vatican City State:

His Eminence Giuseppe Cardinal Caprio, Grand Master of the Equestrian Order of the Holy Sepulchre of Jerusalem with the advice and consent of the Grand Magisterium of the Order and I as Governor General of the Order recognizing the tremendous growth of the both the Eastern Lieutenancy and the Southeastern Lieutenancy of the Order in the United States of America and the consequent burdens placed upon the officers of the Lieutenancies in administering such large Lieutenancies and for the benefit and enhancement of the Order and for the greater Glory of God have determined to establish the Middle Atlantic Lieutenancy of the Equestrian Order of the Holy Sepulchre of Jerusalem in the United States of America.

Therefore His Eminence Giuseppe Cardinal Caprio, Grand Master by personal appointment of His Holiness Pope John Paul II, does hereby create and establish the Middle Atlantic Lieutenancy of the Equestrian Order of the Holy Sepulchre of Jerusalem in the United States of America with the following territorial and geographical jurisdiction:

1. The State of Maryland
2. The State of Delaware

Both states are taken from the Eastern Lieutenancy of the Order in the United States of America, together with

1. The District of Columbia
2. The State of Virginia
3. The State of West Virginia

4. The State of North Carolina
5. The State of Tennessee

from the Southeastern Lieutenancy of the Order in the United States of America.

It is with pleasure that I present the Decree of Appointment as the Lieutenant of the Middle Atlantic Lieutenancy to His Excellency Bernard J. Ficarra, KGCHS.

Additionally, the Middle Atlantic Lieutenancy includes the Archdiocese for the Military Services, U.S.A.

On the evening of May 7, 1994, 50 Knights and Ladies came together for the first time in the Middle Atlantic Lieutenancy to celebrate Holy Mass at St. Anne's Church in Northwest Washington, D.C. The principal celebrant was Rev. Msgr. William E. Lori, KHS, Chancellor and Vicar-General of the Archdiocese of Washington. On that date, His Eminence James Cardinal Hickey, KGCHS, Grand Prior of the Lieutenancy, was called to Rome. Msgr. Lori [now Bishop Lori] graciously relayed His Eminence's message that he was united with us in prayer for the success of this new Lieutenancy. Clearly, a new era had dawned for the Equestrian Order of the Holy Sepulchre of Jerusalem in the capital city of the United States of America.

A highlight of the Liturgy was Msgr. Lori's inspiring homily. It moved each Knight and Lady. In his homily, Msgr. Lori emphasized that at the soul of the Order is "a passionate love for Jesus Christ." It is through our love for Jesus that we are "inspired" to an ardent attachment to Jerusalem, "that privileged place where the Church was born." This faithfulness to the Holy Land is the foundation for our apostolate. "It is our mission to know and understand the challenges, the sufferings, and the needs of our fellow Catholics who count on our concern, our generosity, and our spiritual solidarity as they strive to keep the Faith alive in the Holy Land."

The first investiture of the Middle Atlantic Lieutenancy occurred on the weekend of 5th and 6th November, 1994 at the Basilica

*H.E. Sir Bernard J. Ficarra, KGCHS*

of the National Shrine of the Immaculate Conception in Washington, D.C. With ecclesiastical splendor radiating the charisma of divinely inspired faith, the investiture was a pictorial drama of Catholicism in action. It was an overt manifestation of chivalrous dedication to the Holy Land and all it represents to the world—the greatest event in history, the Incarnation of Our Lord. The Lieutenancy's Grand Prior, His Eminence James Cardinal Hickey, KGCHS, celebrated the Investiture Holy Mass with concelebrants H.E. Archbishop Joseph T. Ryan, KGCHS; H.E. Archbishop Joseph T. Domino, KC*HS, the Ordinary of the Archdiocese for the Military Services; and H.E. Bishop John J. Glynn, KC*HS. Present with H.E. Bernard J. Ficarra, KGCHS, Lieutenant of the Middle Atlantic Lieutenancy, were H.E. Ambassador Count Ludovico Carducci Artenisio, the Governor General; H.E. F. Russell Kendall, Knight of the Collar, Vice Governor General and member of the Grand Magisterium; H.E. Count Aldo Maria Arena, member of the Grand Magisterium; and the Custos of the Holy Land, the Right Reverend Giuseppe Nazzaro, O.F.M. The Homilist was H.E. Archbishop Joseph T. Domino. H.E. Archbishop Joseph I. Ryan, KGCHS, and Lady Jean A. Ficarra, LGCHS, received the Silver Palm of Jerusalem in the name of the Grand Master, His Eminence Giuseppe Cardinal Caprio, for their many years of dedicated service and charitable endeavors in the Holy Land. The Custos of the Holy Land, the Right Reverend Giuseppe Nazzaro, O.F.M., presented to the Lieutenancy's Grand Prior, His Eminence James Cardinal Hickey, KGCHS, the Pontifical Cross of Jerusalem.

In his words of encouragement, H.E. Bernard J. Ficarra, KGCHS, stated:

> To each Knight and Lady of our Order, may the beautiful charity in your hearts move you to emulate Mary and imitate her son, Jesus. Following Christ with admirable zeal will elevate you to heights of holiness through the intercession of our Heavenly Mother Mary, Queen of Palestine. She guides us towards a true love for her divine Son. Through this love we, as Knights and Ladies, are able to shoulder the apostolate that serves Christianity in the Holy Land. If God is with us, no evil can harm us. If we serve God, we shall never be in need. Serving others brings peace of mind. This peace grows in abundance to overflowing joy which we can share with others. The joy of peace begets goodness which overcomes sorrow and gives us strength to carry on against earthly burdens.

The Knights and Ladies of the Middle Atlantic Lieutenancy have prominent leadership in the spiritual orientation of the Equestrian Order of the Holy Sepulchre of Jerusalem in the United States of America. The Lieutenancy's ecclesiastical activities have been concentrated at the Basilica of the National Shrine of the Immaculate Conception, at the Franciscan Monastery of the Commissariat of the Holy Land, and at the Cathedral of Saint Matthew, the Apostle. All are located in Washington, D.C. The annual Ecclesiastic Calendar starts with Lenten prayers including Stations of the Cross, morning recollection, and Sacrament of

Reconciliation. Palm Sunday Mass at the Monastery is followed by Good Friday Mass at the Basilica. The Lieutenancy joins with the Military Archdiocese for rosary and prayer at the Memorial Day Mass. Corpus Christi Mass with Eucharistic Procession and special celebrations in support of the Grand Prior of the Lieutenancy are held at the Basilica. The Triumph of the Cross is celebrated at the Franciscan Monastery along with Conferral of Scrolls. The Ecclesiastical Calendar ends with the Annual Investiture celebrated at the Cathedral of St. Matthew. Additional noted honors were rendered in 1995 to Lady Eleanor Helen Augustine who was elected to the rank of Lady Grand Cross, and in 1996 the Silver Palm of Jerusalem was granted to Rev. Edward Everett Briggs.

At the end of 1997, the Middle Atlantic Lieutenancy had a total of 357 Confreres and Consoeurs, including 63 clergymen, 14 Bishops, 3 Archbishops, and 2 Cardinals.

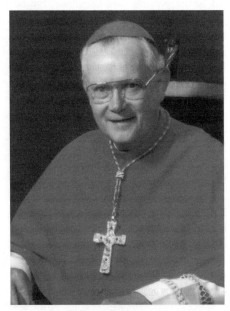

*His Eminence James A. Cardinal
Hickey, KGCHS*
(Bachrach)

# CHAPTER 32

# SOUTHWESTERN LIEUTENANCY: 1986 TO THE PRESENT

The Southwestern Lieutenancy of the Order of the Holy Sepulchre of Jerusalem came into being in 1986 when it was decreed by the Grand Magisterium in Rome that the Southern Lieutenancy was to be divided. At the final banquet of the Southern Lieutenancy held in Corpus Christi, Texas, Sir F. Russell Kendall, later Knight of the Collar, announced that the new Southwestern Lieutenancy was to be made up of the States of Texas, Oklahoma, Arkansas, and New Mexico. Sir Russell also announced that Sir Andrew J. Layden, KGCHS, of Houston, had been appointed to the post of Lieutenant for the new lieutenancy. The Most Reverend Rene

*H.E. Albin J. Brezna*

Gracida, Bishop of Corpus Christi, was to be the Grand Prior. The new lieutenancy started its existence with 970 Confreres and Consoeurs, which was more than the total of the entire Southern Lieutenancy just three years before.

The first annual meeting and investiture for the new lieutenancy was held in Houston on October 24-25, 1987. A total of 72 new Knights and Ladies were invested in ceremonies held in St. Michael's Church. Among those invested were the Most Rev. Robert F. Sanchez, Archbishop of Santa Fe; the Most Rev. Reymundo Pena, Bishop of El Paso; and the Most Rev. Enrique San Pedro, S.J., Auxiliary Bishop of Galveston-Houston. Bishop Gracida invested the new Knights and Ladies, and the Most Rev. Joseph A. Fiorenza, Bishop of Galveston-Houston, was the principal celebrant at the Memorial Mass on Saturday, October 24, 1987, and the Mass of Investiture the following day. More than 700 participated in the two-day program.

At the end of 1990, the Lieutenancy had a total of 1,262 Confreres and Consoeurs including 100 clergy, of which 22 were bishops and 2 were archbishops.

Sir Andrew J. Layden retired in 1995. He was succeeded by H.E. Albin J. Brezna, KGCHS. The Grand Prior is H.E. the Most Rev. Rene Gracida, Bishop of Corpus Christi, Texas.

*H.E. Most Rev. Rene M. Gracida,*
*KGCHS*

# CHAPTER 33

# NORTHERN LIEUTENANCY: 1963 TO THE PRESENT

Late in 1963, but officially in April, 1965, a Northern Delegation of the Order was formed by the transfer to it of twelve states from the Eastern and Western Lieutenancies of the United States. The Western Lieutenancy then became the Southern Lieutenancy. States assigned to the Northern Delegation were Illinois, Indiana, Iowa, Kentucky, Michigan, Minnesota, Missouri, Nebraska, North Dakota, Ohio, and Wisconsin. His Excellency Sir Joe Zach Miller III, KGCHS, was appointed Delegate and then later Lieutenant. His Excellency, Most Reverend Leo Binz, KC*HS, Archbishop of Saint Paul and Minneapolis, was appointed Grand Prior. Seventy-one Knights and 21 Ladies became the nucleus of the Northern Delegation.

In May, 1966, His Eminence John Patrick Cardinal Cody, the Archbishop of Chicago, became Grand Prior. In December 1968, His Eminence John Joseph Cardinal Carberry, Archbishop of St. Louis, was appointed Grand Prior. Early in 1971, Sir Alfred J. Blasco, Knight of the Collar, was appointed Lieutenant. During the administration of H.E. Sir Joe Zach Miller, 1963 to 1970, the total Knights and Ladies had grown to 197. In 1977, His Excellency Sir Herbert M. Adrian, KGCHS, succeeded H.E. Alfred Blasco who had been appointed Vice Governor General. In 1979, His Excellency, the Most Rev. Michael F. McAuliffe was appointed Grand Prior. During Sir Alfred Blasco's administration, the total Confreres and Consoeurs had reached 432. In 1983, with the retirement of H.E. Herbert Adrian, H.E. James E. Madigan, KGCHS, became Lieutenant. During Sir Herbert Adrian's administration, the total number of Knights and Ladies had grown to 787.

In 1986, the Lieutenancy was divided into the Northern and North Central Lieutenancies. H.E. James E. Madigan became the Lieutenant of the North Central Lieutenancy and H.E. Anthony Adducci, KGCHS, was appointed Lieutenant of the Northern Lieutenancy. His Excellency, the Most Rev. Michael McAuliffe continued as Grand Prior of the Northern Lieutenancy. His Eminence Joseph Cardinal Bernardin, Archbishop of Chicago, became the Grand Prior of the North Central Lieutenancy. The original Lieutenancy had a total of 824 Confreres and Consoeurs at the time of the division. The eight states assigned to the Northern Lieutenancy were: Minnesota, North and South Dakota, Iowa, Colorado, Kansas, Missouri and Nebraska.

By the 16th of April, 1989, the new Northern Lieutenancy had 565 Knights and Ladies. The Grand Prior, Bishop McAuliffe, had retired in 1988 and Cardinal Caprio conferred on him the title Honorary Grand Prior. The Archbishop of Dubuque, Iowa, the Most Reverend Daniel W. Kucera was then appointed the new Grand Prior and assumed his responsibilities at the Lieutenancy Investiture in Denver, Colorado on September 26, 1992. The following year, Lieutenant Adducci retired as Lieutenant. He was followed by His Excellency William B. Guyol, KGCHS, of St. Louis, Missouri. Archbishop Kucera remained as Grand Prior.

Archbishop Kucera retired as Grand Prior in 1996. He was succeeded by the Most Reverend Justin Rigali, Archbishop of St. Louis in September of 1996. The Northern Lieutenancy had 973 Knights and Ladies as of the end of 1996.

*H.E. Most Rev. Justin F. Rigali, KGCHS*

*H.E. Sir William B. Guyal, KGCHS*
(Westrich Photography)

# CHAPTER 34

# NORTH CENTRAL LIEUTENANCY: 1986 TO THE PRESENT

The North Central Lieutenancy of the Order came into being in 1986 when the Grand Magisterium in Rome decided that the Northern Lieutenancy was to be divided. The division of the Northern Lieutenancy was announced on July 1, 1986. The states assigned to the North Central Lieutenancy were Illinois, Indiana, Kentucky, Michigan, Ohio, and Wisconsin. Sir James Madigan, KGCHS, was designated as the Lieutenant. His Eminence, the late Joseph Cardinal Bernardin, Archbishop of Chicago, was appointed Grand Prior.

A joint meeting of the Northern and North Central Lieutenancies was held in Milwaukee April 25–26. Separate meetings were scheduled for 1987 in Minneapolis for the Northern Lieutenancy and Detroit for the North Central Lieutenancy.

At the 1990 Annual Meeting in Louisville, Sir James Madigan, KGCHS, announced his retirement as Lieutenant. His Excellency Sir F. Russell Kendall, Knight of the Collar, announced that his successor would be Sir Matthew J. Lamb, KGCHS. Under his leadership, the Lieutenancy experienced consistent growth from 1990 through 1996 with increasing numbers of Knights and Ladies and growth in contributions to the Holy Land.

In 1995, during the investiture ceremonies in Cleveland, Ohio, a "Crusade of Prayer" initiated by the Lieutenancy, was announced with full support by the Grand Master, His Eminence Giuseppe Cardinal Caprio and the Lieutenancy's Grand Prior, His Eminence Joseph Cardinal Bernardin. All Knights and Ladies were asked to pray one decade of the rosary daily for peace in the Holy Land. The purpose being that if there could be peace in the Holy Land, there could be peace worldwide.

Subsequently, in 1996, an historic event for the Lieutenancy took place in Chicago. The first interfaith service consisting of representatives of the Jewish, Muslim, and Christian religions was held during the Lieutenancy's Annual Meeting. His Eminence, Joseph Cardinal Bernardin and newly appointed Grand Master, His Eminence, Carlo Cardinal Furno awarded these leaders the acclaimed Cross of Merit of the Order for their outstanding efforts in the betterment of understanding and cooperation among the different faiths. Consequently, an interfaith "Call to Prayer" was initiated. Knights and Ladies of the Lieutenancy visited churches, temples, and mosques of the Christian, Jewish, Muslim, Buddhist, and Hindu faiths asking them to join with them, by praying in their own traditions for peace in Jerusalem. Lieutenant Sir Matthew Lamb met with leaders worldwide and this message is being spread to over 30 countries. The interfaith service is becoming a tradition that will be practiced annually by the North Central Lieutenancy and hopefully by all other Lieutenancies.

On November 14, 1996, the Lieutenancy suffered the loss of its Grand Prior and devoted adviser, His Eminence Joseph Cardinal Bernardin. Cardinal Bernardin, during the diocesan Annual Mass a month prior to his death, addressed the Knights and Ladies, reaffirming his commitment to the Crusade of Prayer and the Interfaith Service. The Most Rev. Francis E. George, OMI, succeeded Cardinal Bernadin. In early 1998, Bishop George was elevated to Cardinal.

At the end of 1996, the Lieutenancy consisted of 392 Knights, 359 Ladies, 2 Cardinals, 31 Bishops, 79 Priests, 1 Abbot, 1 Brother, and 3 Sisters.

*His Eminence Sir Francis Cardinal George, OMI, KGCHS*

*H.E. Sir Matthew J. Lamb, KGCHS*
(Stuart-Rodgers-Reilly)

# CHAPTER 35

# WESTERN LIEUTENANCY: 1967 TO THE PRESENT

During the late 1960s and early 1970s, Knights and Ladies from western states were inducted into the Order through the Southern Lieutenancy of the United States. As their numbers grew, a Western Delegation of the Southern Lieutenancy was formed in 1967 to provide a measure of local jurisdiction to West Coast Knights and Ladies who, at that time, resided chiefly in California and Alaska. Sir Roger Freeman, KGCHS, was appointed the Western Delegate, and the Most Rev. Leo T. Maher, Bishop of San Diego, became the Grand Prior for the Delegation. The first west coast investiture for the Western Delegation was held in 1970. Fifty seven new Knights and Ladies (a large number at that time) were invested in the Immaculata Chapel of the University of San Diego.

The number of Knights and Ladies continued to grow in the western states. It became apparent that there was a large group of distinguished Catholic men and women in the Western United States who deserved to be recognized for their lives of service to the Church. In 1973, therefore, the Western Delegation became a full-fledged Western Lieutenancy. The Knights and Ladies of the new Lieutenancy totaled 140 taken from the Southern Lieutenancy. The Western states included Alaska, Arizona, California, Hawaii, Idaho, Montana, Nevada, Oregon, Utah, Washington, and Wyoming. Bishop Leo T. Maher was appointed as the Grand Prior of the new Lieutenancy, and Sir William J. Doyle, KGCHS, was named the first Lieutenant.

Under Sir William J. Doyle's distinguished leadership, the Western Lieutenancy flourished. From the original 140 charter Knights and Ladies, the Lieutenancy had grown to 490 by the end of 1983. In 1983 Sir William retired as Lieutenant and was succeeded by Sir John D. Boyce, KGCHS, who had served as treasurer of the Lieutenancy. Bishop Maher continued as Grand Prior. The Lieutenancy continued to grow at an increasing rate so that it doubled in size by 1990 to 1,050 Confreres and Consoeurs of which 910 were Knights and Ladies, and 105 Clergy including 46 bishops. Bishop Maher died in February 1991. His successor is His Eminence Roger Cardinal Mahony, D.D., Archbishop of Los Angeles.

The Grand Master, His Eminence Maximilian Cardinal de Furstenberg visited the Lieutenancy on three occasions. The first time was in 1973 for the inaugural investiture of the new Lieutenancy, and subsequently in 1977 and 1981. The Latin

Patriarch of Jerusalem, His Beatitude James J. Beltritti visited the Lieutenancy in the fall of 1978 in San Diego and in San Francisco. In 1989, the successor to Cardinal de Furstenberg, His Eminence Joseph Cardinal Caprio, visited the Lieutenancy in Palm Springs, California.

In the words of His Excellency F. Russell Kendall, Knight of the Collar: "The Western Lieutenancy had also continued to grow and had retained all of the states in its original jurisdiction." His Excellency John D. Boyce retired after the Investiture and Annual Meeting held in Phoenix, Arizona on October 25–27, 1991. The Grand Master, Cardinal Caprio, then appointed His Excellency Dr. George G. Zorn, of El Cajon, California, as the new Lieutenant. John Boyce had served eight years in office and was made the second Lieutenant of Honor of the Western Lieutenancy.

*H.E. Sir George G. Zorn, KGCHS*

The next year the Annual Meeting and Investiture was held in Anchorage, Alaska, and the group was honored by the presence of two cardinals, the Grand Master Cardinal Caprio, and the Lieutenancy Grand Prior, Cardinal Mahony. Also attending were the Governor General, His Excellency Count Ludovico Carducci Artenisio, and the Vice-Governor General, His Excellency F. Russell Kendall. At this first meeting under the direction of the new Lieutenant, Dr. Zorn, these dignitaries had a special meeting in a beautiful Alaskan cottage owned by Knight and Lady Thomas Carey. By this time, the Lieutenancy had grown to 1,159 Knights and Ladies. Here it was decided that the large area of jurisdiction, approximately three thousand miles north and south and east and west, created an overwhelmingly difficult problem for one Lieutenant and his Council who must "till the field" without compensation but at great expense to themselves, thus the "field" should be reduced in size. Therefore, it was decided that the following year at the Annual Meeting of the Western Lieutenancy in Anaheim, California, the Lieutenancy would be divided into the Northwestern and the Western Lieutenancies. His Eminence the Grand Master, Cardinal Caprio accomplished this on November 7, 1993. His Excellency Dr. George Zorn continued as Lieutenant and His Eminence Cardinal Mahony, Archbishop of Los Angeles, as Grand Prior. The Grand Master then appointed His Excellency Albert E. Maggio of San Francisco, California, as Lieutenant of the

Northwestern Lieutenancy, and His Excellency the Most Reverend John R. Quinn, the Archbishop of San Francisco as the Grand Prior.

The division of this very large territory now gave the Northwestern Lieutenancy jurisdiction over the states of Oregon, Washington, Idaho, Montana, Wyoming, Alaska, and that part of California north of but not including Santa Barbara. This Lieutenancy now includes the following Dioceses in California: the Archdiocese of San Francisco and the dioceses of Oakland, Sacramento, Santa Rosa, Stockton, Monterey, Fresno, and San Jose. The Western Lieutenancy retained these states: Arizona, Utah, Nevada, Hawaii, and that part of California south of and including Santa Barbara. These comprised the Archdiocese of Los Angeles, and the dioceses of Orange, San Bernardino, and San Diego.

On October 28–30, 1994, the Western and Northwestern Lieutenancies had a last joint meeting in Sacramento, the capital of California. The final separation occurred there. At the end of 1996, Knights and Ladies numbered 1009.

*His Eminence Roger M. Cardinal*
*Mahony, KGCHS*
(T. Wilmshurst Photography)

CHAPTER 36

# NORTHWESTERN LIEUTENANCY: 1993 TO THE PRESENT

In the summer of 1992, the Grand Master of the Order, His Eminence Giuseppe Cardinal Caprio; Vice Governor General, His Excellency Sir Russell Kendall; and the Grand Magisterium in Rome gave serious consideration to the division of the Western Lieutenancy of the United States of America. The Western Lieutenancy, at the time, had grown to over one thousand two hundred Knights and Ladies. In addition, the vast expanse of the jurisdiction, approximately three thousand miles north and south, east and west, created an overwhelmingly difficult problem for one Lieutenancy to administer.

At the 1992 Annual Meeting and Investiture of the Western Lieutenancy, held in Anchorage, Alaska, Cardinal Caprio, Grand Master; His Eminence Cardinal Mahony, Grand Prior of the Western Lieutenancy; His Excellency Ludovico Carducci Artenisio, Governor General; His Excellency Sir Russell Kendall, Vice Governor General; and His Excellency Sir George Zorn, Lieutenant, gathered to confer at a special meeting to consider the possibility of a division of the Western Lieutenancy. The final decision was made the following year at the Annual Meeting of the Western Lieutenancy held in Anaheim, California.

The Lieutenancy would be divided into two, the Northwestern Lieutenancy and Western Lieutenancy. His Excellency Sir George Zorn was to continue as Lieutenant of the Western Lieutenancy, together with His Eminence Cardinal Mahony as Grand Prior. The Grand Master appointed His Excellency Sir Albert E. Maggio, a Knight of the Order since 1971 and Councilor for the San Francisco region, as Lieutenant of the newly formed Northwestern Lieutenancy. His Excellency Most Reverend John R. Quinn, Archbishop of San Francisco, was appointed Grand Prior of the new Lieutenancy.

In the division of this very large territory, the Northwestern Lieutenancy jurisdiction now included the states of Oregon, Washington, Idaho, Montana, Wyoming, Alaska, and northern California. The California Dioceses include: the Archdiocese of San Francisco, the dioceses of Oakland, Sacramento, Santa Rosa, Stockton, Monterey, Fresno, and San Jose.

In order to accomplish the transition in a smooth and efficient way, the Western

*H.E. Sir Albert E. Maggio, KGCHS*
*(Vano Photography)*

and the Northwestern Lieutenancy had a joint Annual Meeting and Investiture in Sacramento, California, on October 28-30, 1994. Over 800 Knights and Ladies, together with Bishops and Clergy Knights from all dioceses were in attendance. This final meeting of the entire territory was a very successful joint effort on the part of both Lieutenancies. It was a tribute to the growth and development of the Equestrian Order of the Holy Sepulchre in the Western United States and a fitting beginning for the newly formed Northwestern Lieutenancy.

The official first Annual Meeting and Investiture of the Northwestern Lieutenancy was held in San Francisco, September 29-30, 1995. The Lieutenancy was honored with the presence of His Beatitude Michel Sabbah, Latin Patriarch of Jerusalem; His Excellency Sir Russell Kendall, Vice Governor General; and from the Western Lieutenancy, Lieutenant Sir George Zorn, and Honorary Lieutenants, His Excellency Sir William Doyle and His Excellency Sir John Boyce. The beautiful and stately Cathedral of St. Mary's of the Assumption was the setting for the Investiture Mass and the Memorial Mass for our deceased Knights and Ladies. Promotions and Vigil Service were held at the historic Mission Dolores Basilica. The Westin St. Francis Hotel was the headquarters for the weekend; 250Knights and Ladies were in attendance. The successful Annual Meeting was planned and orchestrated by chairpersons, Sir Robert Begley and Lady Jane Waal, of San Francisco, along with their able committees. The notable success of the first official meeting for the newly formed Lieutenancy was a tribute to the enthusiastic participation of the Knights and Ladies.

Portland, Oregon, was the setting for the Annual Meeting and Investiture held on October 18-20, 1996. The Liturgies were held at the newly renovated and refurbished St. Mary's Cathedral of the Immaculate Conception. His Excellency, Most Reverend William J. Levada, as the former Archbishop of Portland, was the main force behind the renovation and modernization of this beautiful Cathedral. The Archdiocese of Portland celebrated its 150th Anniversary. It is the second oldest Archdiocese in the United States. The newly appointed Archbishop, Most Reverend Francis George (later Cardinal), was a gracious host. The Northwestern

Lieutenancy's Grand Prior, Most Reverend John R. Quinn, officiated at the Annual Investiture ceremony. Honored speakers for this occasion, were the Most Reverend William J. Levada, Archbishop of San Francisco and Monsignor Sir Robert L. Stern, Secretary General, Catholic Near East Welfare Association, New York. It was an outstanding, well-coordinated, successful Annual Meeting and Investiture. The chairpersons for this event, Councilors Sir Arthur and Lady Ruth Schulte, and their committees were highly complimented for all their efforts to make this a successful weekend gathering.

The fruitful progress and growth of the Northwestern Lieutenancy should be attributed to the splendid cooperation of the Officers, the Area Council Members, the Bishops and Clergy, as well as the Knights and Ladies of the Lieutenancy. The number is growing steadily, now 486 Knights and Ladies. All have been most supportive with their annual voluntary contributions. The Lieutenancy has made large contributions to the University, Seminary, Christian Youth Center, and activities of the Patriarchal work in Jerusalem and other regions of the Holy Land. Substantial support of the fund for the restoration of the Della Rovere Palace in Rome is continuing.

With upcoming Annual Investiture Meetings planned for Seattle, Anchorage, and possibly Monterey, and San Francisco, the growth and development of the Northwestern Lieutenancy is assured. The continued support, enthusiasm, and participation of our Knights and Ladies will guarantee the long-term success of the new Northwestern Lieutenancy.

*H.E. Most Rev. John R. Quinn, KGCHS*
(Vano Photography)

# CHAPTER 37

# NORTHEASTERN LIEUTENANCY: 1981 TO THE PRESENT

With almost 2,000 Knights and Ladies in the Eastern Lieutenancy in the early 80s, it was deemed appropriate to consider steps to divide the lieutenancy. It was apparent that the first initiative was to create a New England or Northeastern Magistral Delegation. With many "New Yorkers" living in Connecticut, His Excellency, Sir Alfred J. Blasco, Knight of the Collar, suggested to His Eminence, Maximilian Cardinal de Furstenberg, Cardinal Grand Master, that he be permitted to contact His Eminence, Humberto Cardinal Medeiros, Archbishop of Boston, to discuss a possible Magistral Delegation in the Northeastern United States consisting of the New England States except Connecticut, with headquarters in Boston.

Sir Alfred made an appointment for Sir Louis-Israel Martel, a dedicated Knight of the Montreal Lieutenancy residing in Manchester, New Hampshire, to see Cardinal Medeiros. An interview was graciously given, which made it possible for Sir Louis to acquaint His Eminence with the purpose and accomplishments of the Order. With Cardinal Medeiros and Sir Alfred in Rome at the same time, Sir Alfred invited Cardinal Medeiros to have dinner with him and the Cardinal Grand Master at the Grand Hotel on March 21, 1981. It was there that the Northeastern Lieutenancy was born.

Sir Alfred was invited to a luncheon with Cardinal Medeiros at the Boston Chancery on April 8, 1981. The purpose was to meet the Knight that the Cardinal wanted to appoint as the Magistral Delegate. It was at this luncheon that His Excellency, Sir Norman E. MacNeil, KGCHS, the future Lieutenant of the Northeastern Lieutenancy, met Sir Alfred who was very much impressed with the Cardinal's choice. There followed the setting up of the Northeastern Magistral Delegation with Sir Norman as the Magistral Delegate and Cardinal Medeiros as Grand Prior. The States of Maine, New Hampshire, Vermont, Rhode Island, and Massachusetts were carved out of the Eastern Lieutenancy and assigned to the new Magistral Delegation. Of 163 Knights and Ladies in the new jurisdiction, 62 became the core of the Magistral Delegation with the remaining electing to stay with the Eastern Lieutenancy.

The first Meeting and Investiture of the new Magistral Delegation was held

November 7, 1981. The Cardinal Grand Master, then visiting the United States, was invited to attend, and he graciously accepted. Cardinal Maximillian de Furstenberg participated in the ceremonies as did Vice Governor General Blasco, Knight of the Collar. At the dinner concluding the meeting and investiture, the Cardinal Grand Master was so impressed with the Knights and Ladies and the Magistral Delegate, that he immediately, with Sir Alfred's urging, approved an Order for the Magistral Delegation to become a full-fledged Lieutenancy with His Excellency, Sir Norman E. MacNeil, KGCHS, becoming the first Lieutenant. It was announced that the numbers of Knights and Ladies of the Lieutenancy had reached 135.

*H.E. Sir George T. Ryan, KGCHS*

His Eminence, Cardinal Medeiros was called to his reward by Our Lord in September, 1983. In January, 1984, His Eminence Bernard Cardinal Law, then Bishop of Springfield-Cape Girardeau Diocese in Missouri, became the Archbishop of Boston. Sir Alfred, having known Cardinal Law in Missouri, recommended him as Grand Prior to Cardinal de Furstenberg. Cardinal Law graciously accepted the appointment of Grand Prior.

The Governor General, His Excellency, Prince Enrico Massimo Lancellotti and his wife, Princess Oretta, attended the Annual Meeting and Investiture held November, 1984, in Manchester, New Hampshire. Also in attendance were His Excellency, Sir F. Russell Kendall, later Knight of the Collar, Vice Governor General and his wife, Lady Anne, LGCHS, and the Honorary Vice Governor General, Sir Alfred J. Blasco, Knight of the Collar, and his wife, Lady Kathryn, LGCHS.

The Lieutenancy, under the able leadership of His Excellency, Sir Norman, had made splendid progress by 1988 with the total number of Knights and Ladies at 268. At the end of 1990, Knights and Ladies totalled 383 with 56 clergy Knights that included 8 Bishops and 1 Cardinal.

In June 1995, His Eminence Bernard Cardinal Law, KGCHS, met with Sir George T. Ryan, KGCHS, and suggested that he would like to propose Sir George for Lieutenant of the Northeastern Lieutenancy as H.E. Norman MacNeil, KGCHS, Lieutenant since the initiation of the Lieutenancy in 1981, was planning to retire. Sir

George, a member since 1982, was appointed by H.E. Joseph Cardinal Caprio on October 11, 1995. As Lieutenant-Elect, Sir George and his wife Lady Mary Ryan, LGCHS, traveled with H.E. Norman MacNeil and Lady Phyllis MacNeil, LGCHS, to a number of Investitures in other Lieutenancies for final indoctrination in the ceremonies of the Order. Sir George was installed by H.E. Bernard Cardinal Law, Grand Prior of the Northeastern Lieutenancy at an Investiture ceremony at the Cathedral of the Holy Cross in Boston, Massachusetts, on November 18, 1995.

As a great honor to the Lieutenancy and a personal tribute to His Excellency, Sir Norman MacNeil, KGCHS, was appointed to the Grand Magisterium of the Equestrian Order of the Holy Sepulchre of Jerusalem in October, 1995.

The first issue of the Lieutenancy Newsletter was published in January, 1996, with Sir Dennis Looney, Jr., KGCHS, as Editor. The popular Day of Recollection took place at St. Anselm's in April, and a Mass and reception was held with the local Bishops, Bishop Sean O'Malley, OFM Cap., KC*HS, in Fall River, Massachusetts and with Bishop Thomas Dupre, KC*HS, in Springfield, Massachusetts.

On November 16, 1996, the first Investiture under Sir George's leadership was held for the first time in the diocese of Worcester, Massachusetts. Most Reverend Daniel P. Reilly, KC*HS, Bishop of Worcester was the host. There were 43 new Knights and Ladies invested including Most Rev. John Elya, D.D., KC*HS, Eparch of Newton and head of the Melkite church in the U.S.A., and Most Rev. John McCormack, KC*HS, Auxiliary Bishop of Boston.

As of December, 1996, the numbers of Knights and Ladies in the Northeastern Lieutenancy was 548 with 460 laity and 88 clergy including 14 Bishops and 1 Cardinal.

*His Eminence Bernard Cardinal Law,*
*KGCHS*
(Bachrach)

# CHAPTER 38

# PUERTO RICAN LIEUTENANCY: 1982 TO THE PRESENT

Puerto Rico, an island in the West Indies, is a self-governing commonwealth of the United States of America. The Equestrian Order of the Holy Sepulchre of Jerusalem was established in Ponce, Puerto Rico, on March 25, 1982 as a Magistral Delegation. Dr. Luis F. Sala was appointed Delegate and Most Reverend Fremiot Torres-Oliver, Bishop of Ponce, the Prior. The first Knights and Ladies of the Magistral Delegation numbered nine, mostly from the Eastern Lieutenancy. The Magistral Delegation became a Lieutenancy September 25, 1984. The first Investiture of the Order in Puerto Rico was attended by the Grand Master, Cardinal de Furstenberg, the Governor General, Prince Lancellotti, then His Excellency Vice Governor General Sir Alfred J. Blasco, and His Excellency, now Vice Governor General, Sir F. Russell Kendall, later Knight of the Collar. Dr. Luis F. Sala,

*H.E. Most Rev. Fremiot*
*Torres-Oliver, KGCHS*

*H.E. Dr. Luis F. Sala, KGCHS*

KGCHS, later continues as the Lieutenant and Bishop Torres-Oliver remains as the Grand Prior.

At the end of 1993 there were 46 Knights and 52 Ladies in the Puerto Rican Lieutenancy.

# V

# The Order in the Canadian and Mexican Lieutenancies

*Yet neither sleep, nor ease, nor shadows dark,*
*Could make the faithful camp or captain rest,*
*They longed to see the day, to hear the lark*
*Record her hymns and chant her carols blest,*
*They yearned to view the walls, the wished mark*
*To which their journeys long they had addressed;*
*Each heart attends, each longing eye beholds*
*What beam the eastern window first unfolds.*

*Jerusalem Delivered* by Torquato Tasso (1544–1595)
translated by Edward Fairfax (1560–1635)
Second Book, Stanza XCVII

# CHAPTER 39

# THE ORDER IN CANADA: 1864 TO 1900

The Golden Roster of the Order in the Vatican includes Joseph Antoine Romero Lavallee as the first Canadian invested as a Knight in 1864. In 1881 Count de Premio-Real of Quebec was invested in Rome. Canadian history reveals the Order was established in Montreal in 1882. On April 3rd of that year, four outstanding gentlemen of French Canada were invested into the Order by the Most Reverend Charles-Edouard Fabre, Bishop of Montreal. The four Knights were:

| | |
|---|---|
| Sir Louis-Adolphe Huguet-Latour | Montreal |
| Sir Urgel-Eugene Archambault | Montreal |
| Sir Edouard Murphy | Montreal |
| Sir Pierre-Paul Ernest Smith | Quebec |

The Golden Roster of the Order shows the Investiture year as 1886. It reveals further that 8 additional gentlemen were invested in the same year. Canadian archives show the Investiture as in 1882.

| | |
|---|---|
| Sir Georges Couture | Quebec |
| Sir J. E. Landry, M.D. | Quebec |
| Sir Jean Elic Martineau | Quebec |
| Sir E. Lefebvre de Bellefeuille | Montreal |
| Rt. Rev. Msgr. J. Thomas Duhamel | Ottawa |
| Hon. Sir Georges Landry | Quebec |
| Sir Fabian R. E. Campeau | Ottawa |
| Hon. Sir Charles E. Casgrain | Windsor |

Canadian records reveal the following were invested in the Order prior to 1900:

| | |
|---|---|
| Sir Berthelot | Montreal |
| Sir Heney | Ottawa |
| Sir François Kirouac | Quebec |
| Sir J. A. Langlais | Quebec |
| Sir S. Bingham | Ottawa |

# CHAPTER 40

# MONTREAL LIEUTENANCY: 1926 TO 1990

Formal organization of the Canadian Lieutenancies began with the formation of the Montreal Lieutenancy in 1926. It was on March 14, 1926, when a group of twenty distinguished Canadians were invested in Montreal into the Equestrian Order of the Holy Sepulchre of Jerusalem. His Beatitude Most Reverend Louis Barlassina, Latin Patriarch of Jerusalem, presided in the magnificent Cathedral, replica of Saint Peter's in Rome. Present at the ceremony was His Excellency The Most Reverend Georges Gauthier, Coadjutor Archbishop of Montreal, who became an Honorary Knight Grand Cross. Present also was The Most Reverend Pietro DiMaria, Apostolic Delegate in Canada. Also honored were the Reverend Monsignor Alphonse Deschams, named Honorary Commander; Sir Louis Joseph Rivet, named Knight Grand Cross, who was filling the office of Grand Bailiff of Canada. The Council of the Lieutenancy was formed with Sir Victor Morin, KGCHS, as the Lieutenant and His Excellency The Most Reverend Georges Gauthier as Grand Prior.

In 1937, H.E. Sir Alfred Bernier succeeded H.E. Sir Victor Morin as Lieutenant, and it was in 1947 that H.E. Sir Emil Grothe became Lieutenant. In 1954 Sir Eugene Thibault, M.D., KGCHS, was named Lieutenant. Under his able and wise guidance, the Lieutenancy flourished. For his leadership Sir Eugene Thibault was honored with both the Grand Cross of Merit and the Golden Palm of Jerusalem.

In 1967, H.E. Sir Antoine Charlebois, KGCHS, became Lieutenant. He rendered sterling service including several trips to Rome and visits to the Lieutenancies in the United States. In recognition of his splendid services, he was bestowed the Grand Cross of Merit and the Gold Palm of Jerusalem. It was in Sir Antoine's administration that women were admitted into the Lieutenancy. In 1968, His Excellency Most Reverend Paul Gregoire, Archbishop of Montreal, changed the policy of previous Archbishops to permit women investitures. The Grand Prior, still in office, is His Excellency The Most Reverend Andre-Marie Cimichela, O.S.M., Auxiliary Bishop of Montreal.

In 1974, H.E. Sir J. Albert Bissonnette became Lieutenant. The Lieutenancy flourished and soon became one of the top Lieutenancies in the world. His exemplary devotion to the Holy Land, the many pilgrimages he led, and his outstanding service to the Order resulted in recognition that very few have received. He was honored with the Grand Cross of Merit, the Gold Palm of Jerusalem, and finally the much coveted honor as the first Canadian to be named Knight of the Collar of which there are few in the world including the Cardinal Grand Master and the Latin Patriarch of Jerusalem. It must be known that Lady Monique Bissonnette, wife of Sir Albert Bissonnette, played an important role in the outstanding success of the Montreal Lieutenancy.

H.E. Sir Albert Bissonnette, after seventeen years in office, retired because of ill health and died April 7, 1991. In 1990, H.E. Sir Jean-Pierre Laferriere became Lieutenant. The current strength of the Montreal Lieutenancy is 312, including 125 Knights, 142 Ladies, and 45 Clergy.

*H.E. Most Rev. Andre-Marie Cimichela, OSM, KGCHS*

*H.E. Sir Jean-Pierre Laferriere, KGCHS*
(PhotoGraphex-André Tremblay)

# CHAPTER 41

# QUEBEC LIEUTENANCY: 1929 TO 1990

In the last quarter of the 19th Century, the Quebec Lieutenancy listed several members of the Order including:

Count Sir Premio Real
Hon. Sir A.C.P.R. Landry
Sir François Kirouac
Sir Clement Vicellette

Dr. Sir J.E. Landry
Sir Pierre Paul Ernest Smith
Sir J.A. Langlais
Hon. Sir Georges Couture

It was on September 17, 1926, when Sir Jacques Ernest Coté brought together Knights of four Pontifical Orders—Pius IX, St. Sylvester, St Gregory the Great, and the Equestrian Order of the Holy Sepulchre of Jerusalem—for the purpose of establishing an association of Knights. At a reception then held, Sir Ernest Coté was elected President. Some members of the Equestrian Order of the Holy Sepulchre of Jerusalem received the insignia of the Order from Pope Pius XI during a private audience in November 1927. In 1928 Sir Ernest Coté was elevated to Knight Commander of the Equestrian Order of the Holy Sepulchre of Jerusalem, and in 1929 he was promoted to Knight Commander with Star by the then Latin Patriarch of Jerusalem, His Beatitude Most Reverend Louis Barlassina.

Before the formal establishment of the Quebec Lieutenancy, a group of 17 Knights and 2 Ladies in Quebec City belonged to the Order. On June 4, 1929, the Lieutenancy was formally established at the invitation of His Eminence Raymond-Marie Cardinal Rouleau, then Archbishop of Quebec. In attendance were 20 Knights and 2 Ladies. H.E. Joseph Ernest Coté was named Lieutenant. During his tenure in office (1929-1944), investitures were held at the Archbishop's Palace. Members met several times yearly at the home of the Lieutenant. Up until 1950, members in full uniform participated in numerous religious ceremonies. Annually, a full day was devoted to the Holy Land. In 1938, the Lieutenancy played an important role at the first Canadian Eucharistic Congress held in Quebec. Sir Ernest Coté was motivated to work very hard to increase the spirituality of the Knights and Ladies. He was indeed a man of action and dedication until his death in 1949.

Sir Ernest Coté was succeeded by H.E. Joseph Racine, a prominent businessman. Sir Joseph Racine preferred simplicity and as a result, put an end to public parades. Like his predecessor, Sir Racine held meetings of the membership in his home. His first Investiture was held in the Basilica of Quebec so that the general public could witness the ceremony. He initiated the practice of having a banquet following an investiture to present the new Knights and Ladies to the assembled Lieutenancy. In 1964, Prof. Sir Charles Engel, KGCHS, became the Secretary of the Lieutenancy and thereafter the Lieutenancy showed remarkable progress and development.

In 1970, Sir Joseph Racine resigned because of ill health and was succeeded by H.E. Sir Charles Engel. Sir Charles Engel began immediately to establish a solid financial, legal, and spiritual foundation. The result was a formidable, successful Lieutenancy. He was aided by a lovely Lady, his wife, Lady Edith Engel. Others giving substantial support included Sir Jean-Marie Poitras and Sir Larkin Kerwin. Activities of the Lieutenancy under Sir Charles Engel included:

*H.E. Sir Jacques Coté, KGCHS*
(Wilborn & Associates)

- Four-hour monthly meetings with Mass in St. Louis' Chapel followed by dinner and a lecture with discussions
- A day of recollection during Lent
- An annual fund-raising dinner open to the public benefitting the Catholic schools of the Holy Land

In 1979, the 50th Anniversary of the Lieutenancy was celebrated with His Eminence Cardinal de Furstenberg, the presiding Grand Master of the Order. In 1989, Sir Charles Engel became a member of the Order's Grand Magisterium. Succeeding Sir Charles Engel was H.E. Jacques Coté, KGCHS. The 1990 Investiture was presided over by His Eminence Joseph Cardinal Caprio. At the end of 1990, the strength of the Lieutenancy numbered 101 with 61 Knights, 7 Clergy, and 33 Ladies.

## Grand Priors of the Quebec Lieutenancy

With H.E. Sir J. Ernest Coté: Raymond-Marie Cardinal Rouleau, O.P.,

Archbishop of Quebec; Rodrique Cardinal Villeneuve, O.M.I., Archbishop of Quebec; Most Rev. Georges-Emile Palletia, Aux. Bishop of Quebec and later Bishop of Three Rivers.

With H.E. Sir Joseph Racine: Maurice Cardinal Roy, Archbishop of Quebec and Primate of Canada.

With H.E. Sir Charles Engel: Maurice Cardinal Roy, Archbishop of Quebec and Primate of Canada; Louis-Albert Cardinal Vachon, Archbishop of Quebec and Primate of Canada.

With H.E. Jacques Coté: Louis-Albert Cardinal Vachon, Archbishop of Quebec and Primate of Canada; Most Rev. Maurice Couture, Archbishop of Quebec.

# CHAPTER 42

# TORONTO AND VANCOUVER LIEUTENANCIES: 1956 TO 1996

The Order expanded into Ontario in 1956 under the direction of His Eminence James Cardinal McGuigan, the Archbishop of Toronto. In the fall of 1956, Cardinal McGuigan asked Mr. Alexander G. Sampson, an outstanding Catholic layman in Toronto, to form a nucleus of prominent Catholic men with the purpose in mind of forming a Lieutenancy of the Order in the Toronto Archdiocese. Mr. Sampson held a meeting of these men on September 16, 1956. The first Investiture, marking the founding of the Lieutenancy, was held on May 4, 1957. The vesting prelate was His Eminence James Cardinal McGuigan. One of the investees was His Excellency Most Reverend Francis V. Allen, then Auxillary Bishop of Toronto, who became the Grand Prior of the Lieutenancy.

His Excellency Sir Alexander G. Sampson served as Lieutenant from 1957 to 1962. His successors are as follows:

| | |
|---|---|
| H.E. Paul McNamara | 1962–1966 |
| H.E. John Francis Leddy | 1966–1972 |
| H.E. Wallace Clancy | 1972–1980 |
| H.E. John Kirk | 1980–1984 |
| H.E. Francis McKernan | 1984–1992 |
| H.E. R. Gerald Guest, MD, KC*HS | 1993–Present |

His Excellency Most Rev. Francis V. Allen served as Grand Prior from 1957 to 1965. His successors are as follows:

| | |
|---|---|
| H.E. Most Rev. Philip F. Pocock<br>Archbishop of Toronto | 1965–1979 |
| His Eminence Gerald Emmett Cardinal Carter<br>Archbishop of Toronto | 1979–1990 |
| His Eminence Aloysius Matthew Cardinal Ambrozic<br>Archbishop of Toronto | 1990–Present |

The Toronto Lieutenancy, which is officially known as the Lieutenancy of Canada-Toronto, began to expand into Western Canada. A former secretary of the Grand Master Cardinal Tisserant, Rev. Msgr. Sir Pedro-Lopez Gallo, KHS, who was the Judicial Vicar of the Vancouver Archdiocese, and Sir François Aubert, MD,

KCHS, began to work on the extension into the West in the autumn of 1992. This was approved by His Grace, Archbishop Adam Exner, KC*HS, in the winter of 1993, who became the first Prior of the Section of Vancouver of the Lieutenancy of Canada/Toronto. Sir Francois Aubert became the ignaugurating President. The first Investiture was held in the Cathedral in Vancouver in October 1993. The Section was raised to a Magistral Delegation in the autumn of 1995 with Sir William Whelan, KCHS, as the first Delegate, and under the guidance of Msgr. Sir Pedro Lopez-Gallo as Co-Adjutor Prior. It then had 41 Knights and Ladies. It became a Lieutenancy in the autumn of 1996 with Sir William as the founding Lieutenant. Since its founding on October 1, 1996, the Lieutenancy, which has responsibilities for British Columbia, Alberta, and the Yukon Territories, has been prospering. Its membership consists of 60 Ladies and Knights including clergy.

It is most interesting that the Order began in North America in 1882 by a French Bishop—H.E. Most Rev. Charles Edouard Fabre, Bishop of Montreal—and one of those who were the impetus for expansion to Western Canada was a French Knight formerly from the French Lieutenancy.

In the summer of 1996 the Lieutenancy began another Section in the Eastern part of the Province of Ontario, with His Grace Archbishop Spence as the first Prior and Sir John Clemens as the first President.

The strength of the Toronto Lieutenancy in 1996 was 228, including 110 Knights, 106 Ladies, and 12 Ecclesiastic Knights.

*H.E. Sir R. Gerald Guest, MD, KC*HS*
(Newsome Photography)

# CHAPTER 43

# LIEUTENANCY OF MEXICO NINETEENTH CENTURY TO 1997

The Lieutenancy of Mexico was formally established in 1907 when Don Jose Maria Dominguez came to Mexico City and presented his credentials as Bailiff (now Lieutenant) to His Excellency Sir Don Carlos Rincon Gallardo, Duke of Regla. However, there existed at that time several Knights of the Order having been invested either in Europe or Jerusalem in the last half of the nineteenth century. Records reflect that the first Knight of the Holy Sepulchre in Mexico was Don Jose Y. Linan, Inquisitor of New Spain and Canon of the Collegiate Church of Calatayud, in the ancient Kingdom of Aragon that flourished in the eighteenth century. At that time, knighthood was conferred by the Custodian of the Basilica of the Holy Sepulchre in Jerusalem.

On December 10, 1847, following the reestablishment of the Latin Patriarch in Jerusalem by Pope Pius IX, knighthood in the Order was transferred to the Latin Patriarch—at that time His Beatitude Jose Valerga. It is significant that in 1855, the Archduke Fernando Maximillian of Austria, later Emperor of Mexico from 1864 to 1867, became a Knight of the Equestrian Order of the Holy Sepulchre of Jerusalem. Records show that in the second half of the nineteenth century the following Mexicans became Knights of the Order:

General Sir D. Leonardo Marquez Y Araujo
Most Rev. Pelagio Antonio de Labastida Y Davalos
Sir Don Manuel Hidalgo Y Ensaurrizar
Sir Manuel Y D. Vincente Escandon Y Garmendia
Sir Joaquin Garcia Icazbalceta
Sir Francisco de Arrangoiz

Under the Bailiff (Lieutenant) Sir Don Jose Dominguez, the Order prospered up to 1913. In this period the Lieutenancy gained thirteen prominent Mexicans including four prelates, Most Rev. D. Ramon Ibarra Y Gonzalez, Archbishop of Puebla; Most Rev. D. Jose Arriga Y Gonzalez, Archbishop of Michoacan; Most Rev. Montes de Oca Obregon, Bishop of San Luis; and Most Rev. D. Prospero Ma Alarcon Y Sanchez de La Barqueda, Archbishop of Mexico City.

His Excellency Don Jose Dominguez did much for the Order in his six years in the office of Bailiff but left Mexico when least expected in April 1913. Sir Don

*H.E. Sir Fernando U. Calderon, KGCHS*

Carlos Rincon Gallardo Y Romerdo de Terreros, Duke of Regla, was appointed Bailiff and thus became the representative of the Order for the Republic of Mexico. Sir Don Carlos at the same time received the rank of Grand Cross. A like distinction was awarded Her Excellency Dona Carmen Romero Rubio of Diaz, the wife of General Porfinio Diaz, President of the Republic of Mexico. The wife of Sir Don Carlos Gallardo, Dona Conception Cortina, was given the same insignia.

During the period of the Armed Revolution and due to the two world wars, the Order was adversely affected yet endured the tribulation with a heroic response. In defiance of the religious persecution under the rule of President D. Pascual Ortiz Rubio, a thirty-third degree Mason, Knights of the Order held a meeting in the home of Don Fernando Orvananos Y Quintanilla. The meeting was presided over by the Marques de Guadalupe and resulted in the Knights being imprisoned—fortunately for a very short time.

In April, 1940, the Rev. Monsignor Michael Abraham D'Assemani, Representative of the Latin Patriarch of Jerusalem in America, visited the Lieutenancy. Presiding was the Lieutenant Sir Don Carlos Gallardo and in attendance were constituents of the Lieutenancy. Also in attendance was His Excellency the Archbishop of Mexico; the Rev. Monsignor Rafael Vallejo Macouset, Grand Prior of the Lieutenancy; several diplomatic representatives; and many prominent people. The Knights of the Equestrian Order of the Holy Sepulchre of Jerusalem attended in uniform while others were in evening dress.

The death of Don Carlos Gallardo in 1950 caused his widow to reorganize the Lieutenancy. This was accomplished under Pope Pius XI and the then Archbishop of Mexico, the Most Rev. Luis Maria Martinez Y Rodrigues. In solemn ceremony in the Basilica of Guadalupe, presided over by His Eminence Manuel Cardinal Artega Y Bethancourt, a solemn Investiture took place with the Archbishop of Havana in attendance. Thereafter, the Council of the Lieutenancy was installed. His Excellency Don Juan Laine Y Roiz became the Lieutenant and His Excellency Most Rev. Luis M. Martinez Y Rodriguez, Archbishop of Mexico, the Grand Prior. All investitures were small but of course very solemn. In 1952 a Section was formed in

Guadalajara. In 1963 a Section was formed in Puebla (La Angelopolis). In 1968, His Eminence Eugene Cardinal Tisserant, Cardinal Grand Master, visited Mexico and presided over the Investiture. The Lieutenancy continued to be headed by His Excellency Sir Juan Laine Y Roiz. His Eminence Miguel Dario Cardinal Miranda became the Grand Prior later.

Beginning in 1972 for five years, the Lieutenant was His Excellency Sir Guillermo Barroso Chavez while Cardinal Miranda continued as Grand Prior. Beginning in 1977 for ten years, His Excellency Sir Pablo Campos Lynch served as Lieutenant and His Eminence Ernesto Cardinal Corripio Ahumada, Archbishop Primate of Mexico, served as Grand Prior. Unfortunately, enthusiasm for the Order in a Lieutenancy with such a heroic past waned as the Sections and Delegations fell off in large numbers. An Investiture was finally held in 1980, which was years in preparation and through which only four new Knights were added. Meanwhile, Sections and Delegations practically disappeared, leaving Knights and Ladies isolated from each other as spirituality was diminishing in Mexico City.

The Lieutenancy, greatly revitalized by 1990, was headed by His Excellency Sir Ignacio Urquiza Septien, Knight of the Grand Cross. The Grand Prior was His Eminence Ernesto Cardinal Corripio Ahumanda. At the end of 1990, the Lieutenancy had a strength of 196, including: 84 Knights, 94 Ladies and 18 Clergy, including 6 Bishops.

Sir Alfred Blasco, Knight of the Collar, advised that His Excellency Fernando Uribe Calderon, then KCHS, succeed His Excellency Sir Ignacio Urquiza Septien, KGCHS, as Lieutenant. He was nominated Lieutenant of Mexico on March 21, 1991, and invested in a ceremony on July 26, 1991, by His Eminence, Ernesto Cardinal Corripio Ahumada, KGCHS, Archbishop Primate of Mexico and Grand Prior of the Mexican Lieutenancy. Sir Fernando was raised to the rank of Knight Commander with Star along with the advancement of 17 other Knights and 18 Ladies to various ranks. Additionally, 22 new Knights and 12 Ladies were invested. In 1992, Sir Fernando and his wife, Lady Teresita, were nominated as representatives of the Mexican Lieutenancy to the Second Archdiocesan Synod of the Archdiocese of Mexico.

In June of 1996, there occurred the investiture of His Eminence Juan Cardinal Sandoval Iniguez, KGCHS, and that of the Archbishop of Guadalajara, the Most Reverend Norberto Rivera Carrera, KC*HS, the new Archbishop Primate of Mexico, plus 4 priests, 22 Knights, and 14 Ladies. This ceremony was presided by His Eminence Ernesto Cardinal Corripio Ahumada, KGCHS, Grand Prior of the Mexican Lieutenancy. A second investiture occurred on 22 November of that same year wherein an additional 7 Knights and 4 Ladies were admitted into the Equestrian Order of the Holy Sepulchre of Jerusalem.

Also in November, Cardinal Corripio Ahumada, Cardinal Sandoval Iniguez, Sir Fernando, and Lady Teresita along with two grandsons represented the Mexican Lieutenancy at the Jubilee Celebration of the ordination of His Holiness, Pope John Paul II. They also visited with the Grand Master, His Eminence Carlo Cardinal

Furno, and with the Governor General, His Excellency Count Ludovico Carducci Artenisio.

Three Intendencies have been established:

Intendencia de la Nueva Galici at Guadalajara, Jalisco
Intendencia del Nuevo Leon at Monterrey, Nuevo Leon
Intendencia de la Nueva Vizcaya at Chihuahua, Chihuahua

As of April 1997, the Lieutenancy has a strength of 153, including 72 Knights, 62 Ladies, and 17 Clergy including the Apostolic Nuncio, 2 Cardinals, 3 Archbishops, 2 Monsignors, one Abbot, 6 Canons, and 2 Chaplains.

The Mexican Lieutenancy has been involved in several local humanitarian actions helping 190 poor families with food, clothes, medicines, apostolic work, as well as contributing to the Grand Magisterium in the reconstruction of the Palazzo Della Rovere, and to the Christians in the Holy Land through Rome in accordance with its economic possibilities.

# Epilogue

The Knights and Ladies of the Equestrian Order of the Holy Sepulchre of Jerusalem are indeed modern crusaders. They enjoy the paternal esteem of the Vicar of Jesus Christ and the admiration of all devout Christians. Time was when their work was literally the protection of the Holy Places in the homeland of Christianity and the preservation of the Christian presence in Palestine. Their purpose still includes that sublime mission, but in our day the physical shrines of the Holy Land are also the symbols of those spiritual ideals of ancient Christendom, which Knights and Ladies of the Order are pledged to preserve and to propagate.

Times change and with them the challenges to Christendom have new origins. The battle for Christ and for the sanctity of His shrines is no longer fought with lance and sword. It is fought with the arsenal of the spirit, with resources of prayer, good example, and almsgiving. It is fought no longer in a single corner of the globe, but in every place where truth is assailed, justice is compromised, and Christ is scorned. Knights and Ladies are expected to prove as valiant in the defense of the spiritual battlements of Christendom as did their glorious predecessors.

To the Equestrian Order of the Holy Sepulchre of Jerusalem, the Holy Land is not only a place of pilgrimage but, more importantly, the setting of redemption itself. The Church has never waivered in this recognition nor in the importance of the duty of assuring the Christian presence in that sacred place. The Church has considered the Holy Places as a living part of her tradition and, for the preservation of these same Holy Places, has made untold sacrifices.

The disappearance of the Living Faith in the Holy Land would mean dead memorials. Hence, the Apostolate of the Equestrian Order of the Holy Sepulchre of Jerusalem is the preservation of the Living Faith in the Holy Land. The Equestrian Order of the Holy Sepulchre of Jerusalem does all it can to fulfill this objective by building and supporting schools, churches, and seminaries. This is done by prayers, guidance, influences, and alms, so that as Pope Paul VI of happy memory has expressed in his Apostolic Exhortes, *Nobis in Anima*, "that the witness of the Gospel may be kept alive and the presence of Christ's followers may grow stronger around the Sanctuaries."

The Equestrian Order of the Holy Sepulchre of Jerusalem not only has a validity and legitimate history, but now, by ascertaining and recognizing the spiritual values, stimulates all of its Knights and Ladies to live and act as exemplar Christians. The Equestrian Order of the Holy Sepulchre satisfies the need for a valid and glorious force that esteems and recognizes the mind and spirit in a restless, troubled, and contested world.

**God wills it!**

# APPENDIX A

# KNIGHTS AND LADIES OF THE COLLAR

The distinction of a Collar in Knighthood in early years was conferred upon sovereigns and heads of state. Now in Pontifical Orders of Knighthood, only the Order of Christ continues this tradition. The Pontifical Order of the Golden Spur has only one class of Knight. Its badge, a yellow and gold enameled Cross surmounted by a gold military trophy with a gold spur is worn suspended from a gold collar. These two Orders have no organization as in the case of the Equestrian Order of the Holy Sepulchre and the Sovereign Military Order of Malta. As for the Knights of Malta, a Gold Chain and Star are worn only by heads of state.

The Constitution of the Equestrian Order of the Holy Sepulchre of Jerusalem, as

*H.E. Prince Paolo Enrico Massimo Lancelotti, Knight of the Collar*
(Wilborn & Associates)

approved in 1950, permitted a class of twelve Knights of the Collar in memory of the twelve Apostles. The Collar was to be conferred "upon persons of high stature and of exceptional merit." This rank was due by right to the Cardinal Grand Master and conferred, too, to His Eminence the Cardinal Secretary of State of His Holiness, the Cardinal Secretary of the Congregation for Eastern Churches, and to the Latin Patriarch of Jerusalem as Grand Prior of the Order.

On January 1, 1963, Pope John XXIII approved a new Constitution of the Order, confirming the Order "in the legally constituted condition with all the privileges, faculties, honors, and bylaws as part of a legal entity." It continued the distinction of Knight of the Collar but included Ladies as well. Twelve Collars bearing the name of an Apostle were reserved for ecclesiastic dignitaries of the highest rank. One was reserved for the Cardinal Grand Master and another for the Latin Patriarch of Jerusalem. The Constitution went on to say "other Collars may be conferred on lay personages of the highest status or of exceptional merit."

On November 19, 1967, Pope Paul VI approved a revised Constitution for the Order. It continued the two categories of the Class of the Knights and Ladies of the Collar, the first for clergymen and the second for the laity. Of the laity reference was made to "lay persons of the highest dignity and/or outstanding merit."

On July 8, 1977, Pope Paul VI approved the Constitution now in effect for the Order. As to Knights and Ladies of the Collar, the two categories were eliminated along with the number limit. It continues the hightest rank of the Collar but refers to recipients as follows, "the Collar is conferred on the most eminent persons, ecclesiastic or lay, of the highest dignity, in most exceptional cases." It continues to be due by right to the Cardinal Grand Master and the Latin Patriarch of Jerusalem. This rank is rarely conferred.

| Name | Country | Date Conferred |
| --- | --- | --- |
| Her Majesty former Queen Fabiola | Belgium | May 1961 |
| H.E. Dr. Herman Abs | Germany | Sep 1979 |
| H.E. Sir Alfed J. Blasco | United States | Oct 1982 |
| H.E. Prince Paolo Enrico Massimo Lancellotti | Italy | Dec 1982 |
| H.E. Count Peter Wolff-Metternich | Germany | Dec 1982 |
| H.E. Princess Cecily Zu Salm Reifferscheidt | Germany | May 1983 |
| H.E. Sir Julius Schuster | Austria | Mar 1985 |
| H.E. Count Antonio Alberti Poja | Italy | Feb 1987 |
| H.E. Sir F. Russell Kendall | United States | Mar 1987 |
| His Beatitude Michel Sabbah<br>    Latin Patriarch of Jerusalem | Palestine | Jan 1988 |
| H.E. General Henry De Chizzelle | France | Jun 1988 |
| His Majesty King Juan Carlos | Spain | Sep 1988 |
| Her Majesty Queen Sofia | Spain | Sep 1988 |
| His Eminence Joseph Cardinal Caprio<br>    Grand Master | Italy | Dec 1988 |
| H.E. Sir J. Albert Bissonnette | Canada | Jun 1990 |
| H.E. Count Ludovico Carducci Artenisio | Italy | 1992 |
| His Eminence Cardinal Carlo Furno<br>    Grand Master | Italy | Jan 1996 |
| His Majesty King Albert II | Belgium | Oct 1996 |
| Her Majesty Queen Paula | Belgium | Oct 1996 |
| His Eminence Angelo Cardinal Sodano | Italy | Dec 1997 |

The present twenty living holders of the rank of the Collar are from the following countries:

| United States | 2 |
|---|---|
| Germany | 3 |
| Belgium | 3 |
| Italy | 6 |
| Palestine | 1 |
| France | 1 |
| Spain | 2 |
| Austria | 1 |
| Canada | 1 |
| Total | 20 |

*H.E. Sir F. Russell Kendall,*
*Knight of the Collar*

There are nine deceased Knights who received the Collar:

| Name | Country | Date Conferred |
|---|---|---|
| His Beatitude, Alberto Gori<br>Latin Patriarch of Jerusalem | Italy | Jan 1950 |
| His Eminence, Cardinal Canali<br>Grand Master | Italy | Jan 1952 |
| His Majesty, King Baudouin | Belgium | May 1961 |
| H.E. General Antonio Cerbino<br>Collar of Merit | Italy | Dec 1968 |
| His Beatitude, James J. Beltritti<br>Retired Latin Patriarch of Jerusalem | Italy | Nov 1970 |
| His Eminence, Cardinal de Furstenberg<br>Grand Master | Belgium | Apr 1972 |
| H.E. Sir John Craig<br>Honorary Knight of the Collar | United States | Oct 1973 |
| H.E. Count Cantutti Castelvetri<br>Governor General | Italy | Nov 1973 |
| H.E. Sir Douglas Jenkins | England | July 1986 |

As evidence of the rarity of the conferment of the Collar, only 29 persons have received this distinction since 1950.

# ABSTRACTS
# OF PAPAL DOCUMENTS
# RELATING TO THE ORDER

## Document No. 1—July 23, 1847

Pope Pius IX, motivated by solicitude for the Holy City of Jerusalem and especially for the Holy Sepulchre of Our Blessed Lord, restores the power of jurisdiction to the Latin Patriarch of Jerusalem, who in the future is to reside in his See city. His Holiness directs the Sacred Congregation of Propaganda Fide to draw up a specific instruction to determine the details of the Patriarch's jurisdiction.

## Document No. 2 —December 10, 1847

The Sacred Congregation of Propaganda Fide, in an Instruction delineating the jurisdiction of the Latin Patriarch of Jerusalem, specifies that, "With all the rights that have been otherwise sanctioned for the Knights of the Most Holy Sepulchre and which have been most carefully studied remaining in force, it is decreed that the conferring of rank in this Order pertains exclusively to the Patriarch. He shall, however, use this privilege only in favor of those who are outstanding by integrity of life, who have been worth of merit in the cause of religion, and who manifest other requirements for the obtaining of this honor. The offerings which are made by the Knights, moreover, are to be used in accordance with custom for a house of charity for the Holy Land."

## Document No. 3—January 24, 1868

Pope Pius IX, in an Apostolic Letter, replaces the single degree of Knighthood in the Order of the Holy Sepulchre by three degrees: those of Knight of the Grand Cross, Knight Commander, and Knight. The selection and investiture of all three degrees of Knights is to be made by the Latin Patriarch of Jerusalem acting as the Delegate and in the name of the Holy See.

# Document No. 4—August 3, 1888

Pope Leo XIII approves and confirms the permission given by Pope Pius IX to admit women outstanding in piety, generosity, and zeal for the Catholic cause, into the Order of the Holy Sepulchre. He specifies that these women shall be known as Ladies of the Holy Sepulchre, and that they may be admitted to all three degrees of knighthood and wear the insignia of these various degrees.

# Document No. 5—May 3, 1907

Pope Pius X reaffirms the ranks and the insignia of the various degrees of Knighthood. He reserves the office of Grand Master of the Order to the Holy Father Himself, but reconfirms the privilege of the Latin Patriarch to act as his delegate in the nomination and the conferring of degrees of Knighthood. To give added dignity to the Order throughout the world, and to facilitate its business in various places, he gives permission for some Knights to be selected to act as vicars for the Latin Patriarch in regard to supervision of the Order, and these are to be privileged to wear special insignia. The affairs of the Order are to be conducted during any vacancy in the Latin Patriarchate by such vicars who are stationed at Rome, under the direction of the Cardinal Secretary of State.

# Document No. 6—January 15, 1915

A decree of the Sacred Congregation of the Council, in extending a decree of Innocent X that prohibits the use by Cardinals of symbols of secular honor on their coats of arms, to Patriarchs, Archbishops, and Bishops, specifically excludes the arms of the Order of the Holy Sepulchre from the prohibition.

# Document No. 7—January 6, 1928

Pope Pius XI abrogates the provision of the decree of Pope Pius X that reserves the office of Grand Master of the Order to the Roman Pontiff. He decrees that from now on the Association for the Preservation of the Faith in the Holy Places be joined to the Order of the Holy Sepulchre, and that the one resultant body be governed by the Latin Patriarch of Jerusalem. The Order remains under the benign protection of the Holy See, but the Patriarch is to be permanent Rector and Administrator of the Order, with full and proper right of governance over it, and the faculty of instituting new Knights.

# Document No. 8—August 5, 1931

A decree of the Sacred Congregation of Ceremonies adds the phrase "of Jerusalem" to the official name of the Order, so that it is henceforth to be known as

"The Equestrian Order of the Holy Sepulchre of Jerusalem". The decree further prescribes that the Latin Patriarch of Jerusalem forward the names of new Knights and Ladies to the Section for Apostolic Briefs at Rome for the affixing of the visa and seal to their Diplomas, in order that they may enjoy official recognition.

## Document No. 9—March 2, 1932

The new ceremonial of the Knights of the Holy Sepulchre, abrogating all previous ones, is approved by Pope Pius XI, according to a decree of the Sacred Congregation of Ceremonies.

## Document No. 10—June 16, 1940

Pope Pius XII appoints His Eminence, Nicolo Cardinal Canali, Patron or Protector of the Knights of the Holy Sepulchre of Jerusalem

## Document No. 11—August 15, 1945

Pope Pius XII assigns to the use of the Equestrian Order of the Holy Sepulchre of Jerusalem the Church of Saint Onofrio on the Janiculum, together with the adjoining monastery and Torquato Tasso Museum. The Rector and other clergy of the church are to be appointed by the Holy Father, and the church is to be kept accessible to the faithful.

## Document No. 12—September 14, 1949

Pope Pius XII issues Apostolic Brief "Quam Romani Pontificis" promulgating a special mission, the creation of new grand officers, and statutes regarding Knights of the Collar, new insignia, and decorations.

## Document No. 13—December 8, 1962

Pope John XXIII places the Order under the personal protection of the Holy Father.

## Document No. 14—November 19, 1967

Pope Paul VI delineates the authorities of the Cardinal Grand Master and the Patriarch of Jerusalem.

# SELECT BIBLIOGRAPHY

Asali, E.J., Ed. *Jerusalem in History*. Olive Branch Press, NY, 1990.

*Cathechism of the Catholic Church*, The Wanderer Press, St. Paul, MN, 1994.

*Constitution of the Equestrian Order of the Holy Sepulchre of Jerusalem.* Translated from the original, Tipografia Marconi, Rome, 1977.

D'Assemani, Michael, H.A., *The Cross on the Sword*. Photopress, Inc., Chicago,1944.

Doyle, William J., MD, KGCHS, *Origin, Structure and Present Work of the Equestrian, Order of the Holy Sepulchre of Jerusalem*. Third Edition, Revised. Western Lieutenancy publication, LaJolla, CA, 1990.

Epp, Frank H., *Whose Land Is Palestine?* William B. Eerdmans Publishing, Grand Rapids, MI, 1974.

Ficarra, Bernard J. KGCHS, *The Church on the Hill*. Christendom Press, Front Royal, VA, 1992.

Folsom, Frank M., KGCHS, " Saint Onofrio on the Janiculum." Occasional Papers, 1961. Eastern Lieutenancy.

Hardon, John A., S.J., *The Spiritual Exercises of St. Ignatius of Loyola*. Eternal Life, Bardstown, KY, 1995.

Hirst, David, *The Gun and the Olive Branch*. Future Publications, Maxwell House, London, 1995.

Irani, George E., *The Papacy and the Middle East*. University of Notre Dame Press, Notre Dame, IN, 1986.

John, Robert, *Behind the Balfour Declaration*. Institute for Historical Review, Costa Mesa, CA, 1988.

Kendall, F. Russell, Knight of the Collar, *The Lieutenancies of the United States of America, 1926-1995: The Equestrian Order of the Holy Sepulchre of Jerusalem*. University of San Diego Print Shop, 1995.

McDowall, David, *Palestine and Israel, The Uprising and Beyond*. University of California Press, Berkeley, CA, 1989.

Medebielle, P., S.C.J., *The Diocese of the Latin Patriarchate of Jerusalem*. Jerusalem, 1963.

Pasini-Frassani, Count F., *History of the Military Order of the Holy Sepulchre of Jerusalem*. Heraldic College, Roman Heraldic Institute, Rome.

Runciman, Sir Steven, *A History of the Crusades*. Cambridge Univ. Press, 1951.

Schiff, Zeev and Ehud Yasari, *Intifada*. Simon and Schuster, New York, 1989.

Viorst, Milton, *Sands of Sorrow*. Harper and Rowe, New York, 1987.

# About the Author

Loyalty, diligence, and fidelity have characterized the life of Sir Alfred J. Blasco in his adherence to and love of the Catholic Faith, his devotion to the Equestrian Order of the Holy Sepulchre of Jerusalem, as well as in his distinguished professional career as president and board chairman of financial institutions and as national president of the American Industrial Bankers Association. Sir Alfred is truly a leader, not only of Catholic religious organizations but also in ecumenical affairs throughout the nation.

For many years Sir Alfred served as the distinguished Chairman of the Board of Avila College, Chairman of the Honorary Board of Governors of the Baptist Medical Center. He was chosen "Man of the Year" of the City of Hope Medical Center, Duarte, California. There is hardly any civic, charitable, or business organization in Kansas City for which Alfred Blasco has not been a guiding force.

His lovely wife Kathryn, his daughters, Mrs. Cleo Lowry and Mrs. Robert M. O'Connor, his five grandchildren and three great-grandchildren are his love and the wellspring of his joy and unending energy.

In the Cathedral of the Immaculate Conception, Kansas City in the year of Our Lord 1958, Alfred was dubbed a knight of the Equestrian Order of the Holy Sepulchre of Jerusalem. From that moment Sir Alfred has dedicated his time, his resources, his abilities, his very life to the Order and its objective to sustain the Catholic Faith in the Holy Land. The value of his commitment and the success of his efforts were not unnoticed by the Holy See, and in 1971 he was appointed the Lieutenant of the Northern Lieutenancy of the Order in the United States by His Eminence Eugene Cardinal Tisserant, Grand Master of the Order by appointment of His Holiness Pope Paul VI.

Again in 1977, recognizing the value of his counsel and advice, the then Grand Master of the Order, His Eminence Maximilian Cardinal de Furstenberg raised Sir Alfred to the position of Vice Governor General and a member of the Grand Magisterium, the highest active position ever awarded a member of the Order in the Western Hemisphere. As Vice Governor General, Sir Alfred was required to meet with the Grand Magisterium twice a year. So far, Sir Alfred has made the trip to Rome some fifty times and has attended meetings and investitures of various Lieutenancies throughout the world in discharging his responsibilities as Vice Governor. Upon his retirement in 1986 as Vice Governor General, His Eminence Giuseppe Cardinal Caprio, the then Grand Master of the Order, appointed Sir Alfred the first Honorary Vice Governor General, a title that Sir Alfred now holds.

Recognizing Sir Alfred's fidelity to the Order and his unswerving loyalty to the

Holy See, His Eminence Maximilian Cardinal de Furstenberg, Grand Master of the Order, bestowed upon Sir Alfred J. Blasco, the Order of Knight of the Collar of the Holy Sepulchre of Jerusalem, the ultimate rank of the Order rarely conferred and only upon heads of state and others of the highest merit. Sir Alfred became the first person of the Western Hemisphere ever to receive the highest honor that can be awarded to a member of the Equestrian Order of the Holy Sepulchre of Jerusalem. Not only has Sir Alfred been solicitous for the welfare of the Order in the Western Hemisphere, but he has been an influence for the growth and well-being of the Order in every Lieutenancy of the Order around the world.

His Excellency Sir Alfred Blasco is a recognized authority on the crusades and has given particular attention to the First Crusade led by Godfrey de Bouillon, Duke of Brabant, who wrested Jerusalem from the Seljuk Turks in July of the year 1099. Godfrey shortly thereafter founded the Equestrian Order of the Holy Sepulchre of Jerusalem. In *The Modern Crusaders*, Sir Alfred, who is also an acknowledged historian of the Order, has traced its story through all of its vicissitudes to the present time giving the reader a succinct and compact narrative of the History of the Equestrian Order of the Holy Sepulchre of Jerusalem.

*H.E. Sir F. Russell Kendall*
*Knight of the Collar*
*Vice Governor General*

*H.E. Sir Alfred J. Blasco*
*Knight of the Collar*

# Index